Waiting for the Bluebirds

AN EVACUEE'S JOURNEY THROUGH THE SECOND WORLD WAR

June Matthews

ACKNOWLEDGEMENTS

Imperial War Museum (Camberwell) for permission to use their photographs.

I have received invaluable advice and support on a regular basis from **Dr Cailean MacKirdy**, as he listened patiently to the story as it unfolded.

I thank **Dr Eric Inman**, for his kind permission to use his photographs of Chislehurst Caves and **David Mace** for his certificate of D-Day

Every effort was made through the publishers **A. & C. Black Ltd,** to find the owner of the photograph of Peabody Buildings in 'LONDON, From the Earliest Times to the Present Day' by John Hayes, but without success.

I am indebted to my research assistant **Eunice Drewry,** who not only found things out for me, but who patiently helped me with the computer, deciphered my handwriting and challenged my grammar. Without her support this work would never have reached this stage.

First Published 2009 by Appin Press, an imprint of Countyvise Limited.
14 Appin Road, Birkenhead, CH41 9HH

Copyright © 2009 June Matthews

The right of June Matthews to be identified as the author of this work has been asserted by her in accordance with the Copyright, Design and Patents Act 1988.

British Library Cataloguing in Publication Data.
A catalogue record for this book is available from the British Library.

ISBN 978 1 906205 41 6

This book is for my Grandchildren

Joanna, Christopher, Jonathan and Michael

And those that follow ...

So that they might know a little of their family history.

For Joyce, their mother,

And for my children

Nicola and Alan

So that they might know me a little better.

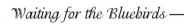

CONTENTS

────────────────────

The White Cliffs of Dover

There'll be Bluebirds over
The White Cliffs of Dover
Tomorrow, just you wait and see.
There'll be love and laughter
And peace ever after
Tomorrow, when the world is free.

The Shepherd will tend his sheep;
The valley will bloom again,
And Jimmy will go to sleep
In his own little room again

There'll be Bluebirds over
The White Cliffs of Dover
Tomorrow, just you wait and see.

Sung by Vera Lynn
'The Forces Sweetheart'
in 1942

PART ONE

1938 to August 1939

THE FOREBODING OF WAR

It was the end of August 1939. The long school holidays were coming to an end and now that I was seven years old, I would be leaving Miss Booth's infants' class to join the big boys and girls in the juniors. I thought it would be all right because I had always liked school especially when I got all my sums right.

These were my thoughts as I went shopping with my mother on that August afternoon. I was holding her hand as we walked along Tavistock Place, and we stopped when we met a neighbour outside Groom's, the paper shop, on the corner of Marchmont Street. The two women talked as I stood eating a banana. Grown-ups' talk was never very interesting, even if you could understand it, and I wasn't really listening.

Gradually I became aware of a sense of anxiety, of fear and foreboding. Mum's voice was strange, quite different from usual and it was as though she were crying.

"It's going to be terrible," she said, "I don't know what we're going to do. It's all in the letter."

Suddenly, I felt scared and wanted to say, "What is it, Mum, what's happened?", but I knew they didn't want me to know, not yet anyway. It was grown-ups' talk. They knew what they were talking about and would not say too much in case I was listening. I felt very frightened but I wanted to hide it from Mum. I knew I must keep hold of her hand and not tighten my grip or give any indication that I was afraid. The best thing to do, I decided, was to carry on eating my banana as though nothing had happened. I took a bite but I didn't really want it. I had a sick feeling in my tummy and I wasn't hungry any more and when you're not hungry, bananas are very difficult to swallow.

* * * * * * * * * *

My secure world was beginning to change. I had been aware of a general feeling of unrest that even a seven year old could not ignore. I heard news bulletins on the wireless but didn't really understand them and I saw newspaper headlines which always seemed to be bad news, but I preferred reading comics. I heard talk of 'the evacuation' but it meant nothing to me. There was turmoil all around us, but it had been like this for a long time. Perhaps the world was always like this and it was how it was meant to be.

I had always felt safe and secure, having complete trust in my mother's loving care. Now, for the first time I began to suspect that these events were going to affect me. I kept thinking of my mother's words "It's going to be terrible, I don't know what we're going to do." Well, if Mum didn't know what to do, and knew it was going to be terrible then things must be really bad.

I started paying more attention to the news, and to the events around me, and tried to make sense of them.

We had had a 'trial blackout' earlier in the month when the lamplighter didn't come round with his oil-lit flame on a pole to light the street lamps, and everyone kept their curtains drawn.

It was very black outside but that was no problem if you stayed in and went to bed, and the next day everything was back to normal. I didn't understand at the time that the whole of London and the south of England had been in total darkness, so that if enemy aircraft flew overhead, carrying deadly bombs, they would not be able to identify their targets.

And why were they collecting blankets? Why did they say on the wireless that they needed twelve million blankets? Lord Woolton broadcast a National Appeal for help on August 29th, saying that they needed six million blankets for the Army, two million for the hospitals and more than four million for the evacuation reception areas.

GAS MASKS AND RATION BOOKS

Then there were the gas masks. We had to go to school to get these and we sat in the hall while they explained how important they were. I knew all about gas – we had a gas cooker and the light in the kitchen was gas. Someone had to stand on the table, and strike a match to light it. When the gas went out, you had to put a penny in the meter which was just inside the door above the coal box. There was a gas lamp on the wall in both bedrooms, but these didn't work, so at night, we had to use the torch.

I knew that gas was very dangerous, and you had to make sure the cooker was turned off and that the baby didn't try to turn the taps on. Sometimes, if it had not been turned off properly, you could hear it hissing and smell it, and it was very unpleasant. If it got left on accidentally there would be a big bang when Mum lit the gas and it was very frightening. I thought of this when they gave out the gas masks, but I didn't tell anyone.

We went into the school hall and they gave us a cardboard box and told us to sit on the floor.

"Open your box," said the teacher, "and take your gas mask out very carefully. Now, hold it by the straps, this way up." The teacher demonstrated how to put the mask on and then asked for a volunteer. "Who'd like to come out and show us how easy it is to put on a gas mask?" A lot of the children put up their hands, and Jimmy Sullivan was chosen to go out in front.

He had to put his face into the mask, and press the rubber against his face. Then he had to pull the straps over his head. We watched this performance with eager anticipation. It would soon be our turn.

"Well done, Jimmy." said the teacher, "Now you can all put on your masks". We had to put them on carefully like Jimmy had shown us and had to practise breathing in and out. When you breathed in, the mask fitted tightly against your face, but when you breathed out, the air came out at the sides against your cheeks and you could feel the rubber flapping as it made a rude noise like blowing a raspberry. They were really quite funny. It was like a game and we were not aware of the seriousness of the exercise.

Following the use of mustard gas in the First World War, with devastating effects, it was believed that gas would again be a major weapon. It was important that everyone was issued with a gas mask and knew how to use it correctly. They even had one for the baby, but his had a Mickey Mouse face so that he would think it was a toy and wouldn't be frightened. We were told that we had to carry them with us wherever we went, and be ready to put them on quickly when we were told to. We didn't realise that our lives may have been in danger, and that someone would want to kill us.

There was other evidence of preparation for anticipated enemy attack. Enormous barrage balloons were flying above London, floating like big silver-grey elephants high in the sky. They were to be a deterrent for any low-flying aircraft whose wings could be caught in the web of heavy cables which anchored the balloons to the ground in parks and open spaces.

And why did they have sandbags everywhere? They were stacked up against the sides of many buildings, making an extra wall on the outside.

At night, searchlights swept the sky, the beams criss-crossing each other ready to track the path of an invader. Air-raid sirens were installed on rooftops, practising their wailing warning drone, and then the uninterrupted welcome all-clear siren.

The plane trees in the yard had been cut down and they were building a large air-raid shelter. The new pink bricks contrasted sharply with the smoke-blackened bricks of our Victorian block of flats. Looking down on the shelter from our window, as they were building it, you could see the thickness of the walls, and the corridors and rooms which would be inside.

We had been issued with ration books with instructions on how to use them, and we all had Identity Cards. My number was DFJA 21/6.

All this activity had been going on around us all the time with a sense of urgency, but I didn't feel threatened in any way. My daily life seemed to go on as usual and I felt safe and secure as long as I was with my family.

Dad was always there, very much the Head of the Family, but it was Mum, the best Mum in the world, who really looked after the three of us – John, aged 10, Basil, the baby, almost two years old and me, the only girl.

The author (aged 7) with brother John   *Basil (aged 18 months)*
in 1939 before evacuation

I had everything I needed. I loved going to school in Herbrand Street – Christ Church, Junior Mixed & Infants, and Miss Booth was a wonderful teacher. I went to Sunday School, and I had joined the Brownies. I felt very smart in my Brownie uniform, complete with brown woolly hat, with a badge sewn on my dress, showing that I was in the 'Imps' patrol.

I had lots of friends and life was good. Now I knew that something was going wrong. Mum's words kept coming back into my head. "I don't know what we're going to do – it's going to be terrible".

OPERATION PIED PIPER

Plans had been made for the evacuation of children over the age of five, from London and other potential target areas. The government had been responsible for the overall plan under the direction of Sir John Anderson. He had masterminded the whole operation to move more than three million people from the potential bombing targets, to the designated 'safe areas'. It was to be the greatest movement of people recorded in the history of this country. The majority of those to be evacuated were children and the exercise was code-named *'Operation Pied Piper'*.

The local authorities were responsible to the government for the arrangements in their own area, and in London this was the London County Council (L.C.C.). The leader of the Council was Herbert Morrison and much of the information was channelled through the schools.

Parents were given information about the plans with a list of things the children should take with them. They were advised to pack only the absolute minimum as the children would have to carry their own bags on the journey – some warm clothing, nightwear and a change of underwear. Other things could follow later.

The London County Council had issued these guidelines for the evacuation:

CLOTHING

Besides the clothes which the child would be wearing (and such should include an overcoat or mackintosh), a complete change of clothing should be carried. The following is suggested :-

Girl	*Boy*
One vest of combinations	One vest
One pair of knickers	One shirt with collar
One bodice	One pair of pants
One petticoat	One pullover or jersey
Two pairs of stockings	One pair of knickers
Handkerchiefs	Handkerchiefs
Slip and blouse	Two pairs of socks or stockings
Cardigan	

Additional for all

Night attire; Comb; Plimsolls; Towel; Soap; Face-cloth; Tooth-brush; and, if possible, boots or shoes and plimsolls.

Blankets need not be taken.

Head teachers are at liberty to utilise, during needlework lessons, material for the making of clothing, small bags, towels, etc. for the benefit of the children, particularly those whose parents are poor. Such articles, except those sold to pupils or otherwise disposed of to pupils in accordance with regulations, should be regarded as official property.

The luggage must not be more than the child can carry. Other clothes needed can be sent later on. The luggage should include the child's identity card and ration book, the gasmask must be carried separately.

E.M. Rich – Education Officer. LCC 1939

It was suggested that a favourite teddy bear or doll should be included to provide some degree of comfort. Packing should be completed immediately and everybody was on 'standby' awaiting further instructions.

It was not compulsory for parents to send their children, but they were put under emotional and psychological pressure – 'Our children are the future of this country. If you really love your children you will want to send them to a place of safety. You owe it to them to think of their future.'

Some families were able to make private arrangements and children were sent to relatives or friends in the country or even abroad. For the rest, it was assumed that parents would co-operate with the government scheme, particularly since the evacuation was being organised through the local schools, most of which would then be closed. There was really no choice.

At the other end of the line, in the reception areas, participation was not voluntary.

"It is of vital importance to preserve the lives of children, who will be the citizens of the next generation. So householders in safe districts must take them in.

PARLIAMENT HAS GIVEN POWERS TO BILLET THEM
COMPULSORILY IN THE RECEPTION AREAS AND THE
GOVERNMENT IS DETERMINED TO USE THOSE POWERS
IF NECESSARY."

Sir Warren Fisher
Daily Mirror – September 4th 1939

Billeting officers were appointed whose job it was to visit all the homes in their area to establish the number of available places.

"You can take two in this room", they were told, "I'll put you down for two of the same sex."

or

"There's room for a camp bed on the landing – have you got a camp bed? No? We'll provide one, and some blankets."

"You'll be paid, you'll get ten shillings and sixpence a week for the first evacuee and eight shilling and sixpence for any others."

The L.C.C. had foreseen that there might be a problem in placing working-class children with infections, sores, head lice, etc. into middle class homes, and prior to evacuation they had opened special cleansing centres for children to attend.

"THE COUNCIL'S TREATMENT CENTRES AND BATHING
STATIONS FOR CHILDREN ARE OPEN, AND MOTHERS
WILL FIND THERE NURSES WHO GIVE EVERY HELP. IF
YOUR CHILD HAS SORES OF ANY KIND YOU SHOULD
AT ONCE SEEK MEDICAL ADVICE, AND IF THERE IS
DIFFICULTY IN GETTING RID OF ANY INFECTION OF

THE HEAD YOU SHOULD SEEK HELP AT ONCE AT THE
BATHING STATION."

The aim, however, was simply to get the children away.
Billeting Officers had been sworn in, none of whom were women,
and their job was to find accommodation in the safe areas.

The only criterion used was space.

At the end of August, when war seemed to be imminent,
the decision was made to implement the evacuation procedure.
Herbert Morrison addressed the people of London through all
the London newspapers. In his message to those concerned, he
appealed directly to both the children and their parents. To the
children he wrote:

> 'With your teachers and friendly helpers you are
> going to the country, where the government
> considers you will be safer than in London if
> war should come. London children are cheerful.
> I want you to be cheerful and friendly on the
> journey and when you get to the other end. It
> is a big task to move you all; so please do all you
> can to help make things run smoothly. Above
> all, be kind to each other. Help each other in
> any little difficulties that may arise.'

Herbert Morrison, County Hall, August 1939

He concluded, anticipating some difficulties and snags, by
endeavouring to raise morale of everyone involved by saying:-

".....as many of your fathers used to sing, 'Pack up your troubles in your old kit bag and smile, smile, smile'. To all those evacuated and to those going with them – Good luck! And a safe return to dear old London."

Herbert Morrison

* * * * * * * * * *

The time had come for Mum to tell us.

"I don't know if you've both heard," she said to John and me, "there might be a war soon and it would be better if you both went away for a while, to a safer place."

"Where are we going?"

"Well, we don't actually know yet, but all the children from your school are going together and some of your teachers are going with you. They will look after you, and you will both be together."

"What about the baby, is he coming with us?"

"No, he's not old enough. He's not two yet and he wouldn't be able to carry his bag. They are going to make special arrangements for the little ones and I shall have to go with him."

"When are we going?"

"Well, we don't know exactly when it will be, but I think it will be quite soon."

"And will we be coming home again afterwards?" I asked.

"Yes, when the war's over, and we hope it won't be too long. And they've said you can take a dolly with you, to keep you company, so would you like to go to the shop and choose one?"

"Oh yes," I said, "I'd like a new dolly. Can I have one which shuts its eyes and goes to sleep?"

"Well, we'll see," said Mum, and I knew that meant 'yes'.

'Rosalyn' had pink cheeks and blue eyes and she came in a big box with a cellophane lid, so that she could see out. When you tipped her backwards she shut her eyes. You couldn't comb her yellow hair because it was stiff like a pot scourer and the comb got stuck. But Rosalyn was beautiful and we were both ready to be evacuated.

We didn't have to wait very long. On Thursday 31st August a directive came from Sir John Anderson at 11 o'clock in the morning, saying simply "Evacuate Forthwith".

* * * * * * * * *

PART TWO

September 1ˢᵗ – September 3ʳᵈ, 1939

'And the Piper advanced and the children followed.'

The Pied Piper - Robert Browning

THE EVACUATION

"Evacuate Forthwith!" Friday September 1ˢᵗ was 'E' Day
– Evacuation Day. Hitler was continuing his relentless invasion of
Europe and was now invading Poland. We were on the threshold
of the Second World War, and if England declared war against
Germany, central London would be vulnerable to enemy attacks
and in particular the main line stations would be prime targets.
The country could be brought to a standstill if the communication
network was destroyed. Herbrand Street, where I lived was not
more than half a mile from Euston Road with three main line
termini, Euston, St. Pancras and King's Cross in a row.

Everyone was ready. The country had been 'on standby'
waiting for instructions to put Sir John Anderson's 'Operation Pied
Piper' into effect. Coaches and buses were ready. Trains were
waiting. Bags were packed according to the list of requirements
issued by the Authorities and the greatest movement of people ever

recorded in our country's history was about to begin. Children from the age of five years were to be evacuated from cities and towns to safe areas. Parents did not know where their children were going, nor for how long.

Daddy kissed me goodbye. "Be a good girl," he said, "we'll see you again soon."

"Come on", said Mum, "or we'll be late."

There was an air of bewildering excitement and anticipation as we made our way to the meeting place at Christ Church School in Herbrand Street. A crowd had gathered on the pavement outside the school and many of my classmates were already there. I was eager to meet my friends and to show them Rosalyn, I was sure they would be very impressed. I was going to watch their admiring faces as they looked at her, and just when they were beginning to lose interest, I was going to tip her backwards and make her go to sleep. They would be very envious. I was not prepared for Rosalyn having some very unfair competition.

There was a new girl! Pat Middlemass was sitting on the windowsill surrounded by curious admirers. She was like a film star in the limelight, looking down on her fans. We were all wearing our coats, as we had been instructed, but Pat was wearing a pretty pink dress and she looked very clean. She was the centre of attention and nobody was interested in Rosalyn. Pat usually went to a private school but the government scheme for evacuation was being organised through the state schools so Pat was coming with us.

We went into the school hall where our names were called and we were put into groups. We were given two big luggage labels on long strings. One was put round our neck and the other one was tied to our luggage. On the labels were written our name, our school and the local authority.

LABELS

Two linen labels supplied with string should be provided for each child. One of these should be worn loosely around the child's neck and tucked under the upper garment, and the other should be fixed to his luggage. On one side of each label should be written the name of the child and the school address; the "school address" will be the address of the school with which the child is travelling. On the other side of the label should be "L.C.C." and the school number in bold figures. Labels will be supplied on request to the Chief Office of Supplies, L.C.C. Supplies Department, 31 Clerkenwell Close, E.C.1.

E.M. Rich – Education Officer. LCC 1939

Parents were told that they would be advised of our safe arrival at our destination as soon as we were settled, and that they would be able to write to us and visit us.

Outside the school, buses and coaches were waiting to take us on the first stage of our journey. Parents were anxious, worried and tearful but tried to be re-assuring to the children. We were confused, bewildered and excited. It was a bit like when we went on our Sunday School outing to Hampstead Heath, although this time there were more of us and we did not know where we were going. Our teachers, Mr Dunkley and Mr Payne, were coming with us.

Mum kissed me goodbye and said "Be a good girl and mind you both stay together." I climbed on the first coach, eager to get a seat by the window so that I could wave goodbye.

Nobody explained that this journey was to take six years, that we would be living with complete strangers and would seldom see our parents or younger brothers and sisters during that time. Nobody told us that we would be leaving the tenement buildings, the grey streets and the smoky traffic for the country lanes, the green fields and the cows. And nobody told us that there would be no bananas for six years because, of course, they didn't know.

We waved goodbye to our families, as children all over the country were waving goodbye. War means separation. Young men were being conscripted into the armed services, and mothers were saying goodbye to their sons. Husbands were leaving their wives, fathers were leaving their children. Separation was the order of the day, and not all would return. The mood of the nation was captured in the popular song which was being sung or whistled everywhere:

Wish me luck as you wave me goodbye!

Cheerio, here I go, on my way

Wish me luck as you wave me goodbye!

With a cheer, not a tear, make it gay

Give me a smile, I can keep all the while

In my heart while I'm away

'Til we meet, once again, you and I

Wish me luck as you wave me goodbye!

The coach took us to King's Cross. Parents were not allowed inside the station. Some had arrived hoping to be able to go on to the platform for a final farewell and to wave goodbye as the train pulled out, but there were lines of policemen and barriers outside the station to keep them out.

Inside, it was crowded with groups of evacuees from other schools, and it was very noisy. Loudspeakers were directing groups to the right platforms and people were shouting. Doors were being slammed and whistles blown. Trains were hissing steam and belching smoke and the air was filled with coal-dust and soot, creating that unmistakeable smell of steam engines.

The teachers were continually checking the group as though we were a flock of sheep and none must stray from the flock. I was in Mr Payne's group.

"You must all stay very close together," he said. We were in twos and had to hold hands.

"Don't let go of your partners, we don't want to lose anyone, do we?" I held John's hand. I didn't want to get lost. I'd been lost once before when I was in the park with Mum and Grandma, and I was taken to the Park Keeper's hut until Mum came and found me. The Park Keeper gave me a biscuit and I was not really frightened, but I was glad when she came. Getting lost here would be much worse. It was so crowded and all the groups looked the same – boys and girls wearing coats with labels and carrying gas masks. I was going to stay near Mr Payne.

All the grown-ups were wearing armbands, and those who were in charge of a party had to wear two, one on each arm.

ARMLETS

All adults must wear armlets. Leaders of parties must wear one on each arm; all others one on the left arm only. Armlets should be made in the schools. They are to be white material, five inches wide, and should bear, in bold red lettering, "L.C.C." and, in black, the school number.

Head teachers who have megaphones may find them useful. In any case school whistles should be taken.

E.M. Rich – Education Officer. LCC 1939

Stewards were holding clip-boards, answering questions and ushering groups in the right direction until finally we ended up on a train.

The compartment was small and narrow with no corridor or central gangway. There were two long seats on each side with enough space for ten or twelve people to sit comfortably, but we were packed in with no room to move. There were more than twelve of us and we were squashed together. "Do not open the windows or touch the door handles," warned Mr Dunkley as the train pulled slowly out of the station.

At last we were on our journey.

The train slowly gathered speed clicking its way over crossing tracks with an ever-changing view of the world outside; over bridges, under bridges and through long dark tunnels. There were sheep and cows in the fields, and sometimes a tractor. We went through stations where we didn't stop and sometimes we stopped where there was no station. We were a very, very long way from home, and I wondered how much farther we were going.

I thought about Mum and Dad at home, and wondered what they were doing. If they looked out of the window of 8A Peabody Buildings, they wouldn't see any grass. All you could see from our three windows was the high, grey wall of 'H block', hiding the sky and keeping out all the sunlight.

Peabody Buildings had been built about 1870 with money given by an American philanthropist, George Peabody, for the

RELIEF OF THE POOR

JOHN HAYES   A & C BLACK LTD

PEABODY DWELLINGS IN HOLBORN,
built in about 1870

When a rich American banker named George Peabody presented half a million pounds to the city of London, the money was used for the same purpose, and the first blocks of Peabody dwellings were opened in Spitalfields in 1864.

relief of the poor. And we were poor. Dad was one of the many unemployed during the recession of the nineteen thirties. He had his 'dole' money, but it did not compare with today's unemployment pay and social security benefits. Sometimes I went with Dad to the Labour Exchange in Penton Street to queue up for our meagre hand-out. It seemed the natural thing to do, and I often saw my friends in the queue with their fathers.

Mum was working – there were always menial jobs for women but they were very poorly paid and even with their combined incomes it was not always possible to make ends meet.

Before moving into Peabody, we had often found it difficult to pay the rent and we were always on the move. Dad would come home sometimes saying "I've found somewhere cheaper to live. Pack your bags as quick as you can and let's get out of here."

It was a case of 'grab what you can, and run', and often things were left behind. The new rooms had probably been vacated by another family on the run avoiding their rent arrears. The 'moonlight flit' was quite a common occurrence during the thirties and was reflected in the popular song: -

We had to move away
'Cos the rent we couldn't pay.
The moving van came round just after dark.
There was me and my old man,
Shoving things inside the van,
Which we'd often done before, let me remark.
We packed all that could be packed
In the van, and that's a fact.
And we got inside all that we could get inside.
Then we packed all we could pack
On the tailboard at the back,
Till there wasn't any room for me to ride.

My Old Man said "Foller the Van"'
"And don't dilly dally on the way".
Off went the van with me 'ome packed in it,
I follered on with me old cock linnet.
But I dillied and dallied, dallied and I dillied,
Lost me way and don't know where to roam.
Oh, you can't trust the Specials like the Old Time Coppers,
When you can't find your way home!

For a while, Dad worked with his parents in the off-licence in Theberton Street, near the Angel, Islington, and in the café in Regents Park Road, but he could find no way of supporting his family. With some financial help from his parents, he tried his hand at business, but all his efforts failed.

We had a café in Pentonville Road, just over half a mile

from King's Cross, and much of the business was from coach drivers who enjoyed Mum's home cooking. She did all the work – the cleaning, the washing-up and waiting at table. The café was very big, and there was an old billiard table at the end of the room, and Dad played billiards with the customers, saying that it was important to keep the customers happy. He kept them happy, and business flourished – until a new coach station was opened down the hill at King's Cross with better facilities for the drivers. No doubt the previous owner saw the red light when plans for the new coach station were approved, and decided to sell. The café was doomed to failure.

The greengrocer's shop in Brixton Road near the Oval was another unsuccessful business venture in 1933. Dad used to go early to the vegetable market in Covent Garden but he had no experience in the retail trade and couldn't make a living.

When we left there, we had nowhere to go. Dad and John went to live with Granddad and Grandma in Islington, and I went with Mum to Auntie Lizzie's. We were living in one room which was infested with mice. I was a toddler, about a year old, and have often been reminded that I chased a mouse round the room trying to catch it.

I was blissfully ignorant of all this turmoil around me, being too young to be aware of the situation, and thriving in the loving care of a wonderful mother. It was hard for Dad, and degrading, but the heaviest burden fell on Mum who, despite everything, gave us all the love and comfort we needed.

The saddest occasions for her were the inevitable unwanted pregnancies. Dad always knew someone who could solve the problem, for a price, and Mum was taken to a gypsy woman who would 'get rid of it'.

Mum had no proper home, and not enough money for the existing family. Dad was insistent and she had no choice, but she bore the burden of this guilt for the rest of her life. She was able to talk to us about it in later years. Basil spoke to me about it quite recently. "Of course, you know don't you, that sadly some of our brothers and sisters didn't make it."

"I know," I replied, "Mum told me. We are the lucky ones that got away."

Our nomadic existence came to an end when we got a two-roomed flat in Peabody Buildings and we were grateful. It was in Herbrand Street near Russell Square on the top floor of 'E Block' and later, three rooms in 'A Block' at No. 8. Thanks to the kindness and generosity of George Peabody, the rent was affordable. It was ten shillings and a penny per week, (50p) including rates.

Our rooms on the first floor looked out on to the grey windowless wall of 'H Block', which blocked out the sun and the sky. Some of the flats had a better view than ours, looking across the yard where we played, or facing the road. But wherever you looked from Peabody windows, there was no grass.

Now, as the train trundled along, I was looking at grass and trees, rivers and farms, sheep and cows, and I wondered how much farther we were going.

The train stopped at Hitchin, in Hertfordshire, and with much excitement we prepared to get off the train.

"Don't touch the door handle," said Mr Payne, " I'll open the door when we've stopped. Pick up your bags, don't leave anything. Make sure you've got everything."

We climbed down on to the platform. "Find your partner, and line up, holding hands," and he checked to make sure we were all there.

"We're going on another train," he told us, "it's a branch line on another platform."

Mr Dunkley led the way and Mr Payne brought up the rear.

The branch line train was not so comfortable, it had wooden seats, but it was not so crowded and we had plenty of room to spread out. It was a slow train but we didn't have very far to go. It rattled along, like a goods train until we got to Baldock.

"Don't forget anything," warned Mr Payne again, "Line up with your partner on the platform and follow me."

Outside the station, a bus was waiting for us, which headed up the Great North Road.

"Now listen carefully. Some of you will be getting off at

Radwell, and the rest of you are staying on the coach to go to other villages. Listen carefully for your name."

We listened carefully.

"Ruth Prater, Pat Middlemas, Doris Van der Wheel, Peter Marshall, Jean Hanwell, Joan Bovingdon, Roy Bovingdon, John Matthews, June Matthews ….."

This was it. The journey was over. We had arrived.

ALLOCATION OF BILLETS

It had been a long journey and I wondered if Mum and Dad would ever find their way if they wanted to come and see us. I hoped they would know which trains to catch and which stations to get out at. And there would not be a bus waiting for them at Baldock. They seemed to be a very long way away.

The coach stopped outside the Village Hall, and the doors were open.

Some of the ladies from the village were already there waiting for us. Inside, the hall was dark green at the bottom and pale yellow at the top. There was a stage at the far end with stairs at each side, like the school hall, and there were chairs around the edge.

The billeting officer had a list, and he was in charge. "When I call your name, you can sit down," he said.

The Village Hall

He started reading the names until he got to ours. "Now, can we have John Matthews and Roy Bovingdon," he said. The two boys raised their hands. "You two boys are going together, please sit there. And June Matthews and Joan Bovingdon – you two girls are going together." Joan and I were told to sit next to each other.

"We're just waiting now for Mrs De Zoote," said the billeting officer. "She has the farthest to come from the Mill House." We couldn't start without Mrs De Zoote.

We looked at the ladies from the village and they looked at us. Some of the ladies were wearing pinafores over their dresses – full-length sleeveless wrap-overs, with a matching belt. One lady was wearing hers without a dress underneath. She had no sleeves and you could see her thin shoulders. I didn't like the look of her.

"I hope we don't get the one with the bony shoulders," I said to Joan, and she knew who I meant.

Mrs De Zoote arrived. It was quite clear that she was the most important lady in the village and she was top of the pecking order. The billeting officer spoke to her briefly and she looked around at us all. "I'll take that one," she said, nodding toward Pat Middlemass. Pat looked as though she had won the raffle, and she smiled prettily as she went to join Mrs De Zoote.

The next choice went to Mrs Walker, the farmer's wife. And so on, each in turn taking her pick until there were only four of us left, and two ladies, Mrs Edwards and the lady with the bony shoulders.

Mrs Edwards was a big lady with her grey hair in a bun and she looked quite old, but she had a very kind face. She looked at the four of us remaining, and said "I'll take the two boys."

John and Roy picked up their bags to go with her, leaving Joan and me to go with the last lady . "You're both going with Mrs Wyant," the billeting officer said to us, "I'm sure you'll be alright when you've settled down." Perhaps they could all see from the expression on my face that I had no intention of settling down.

I didn't want to go with her but I had no choice. All my friends had gone, my brother had gone and I suddenly realised that I had left Rosalyn on the bus and she was on her way to another village. I felt really miserable. This was far worse than being lost in the park and I knew I wouldn't be waiting in the Park Keeper's hut, eating biscuits until Mum came to find me.

It had been a long, tiring and exciting day but I had had enough of it and I wanted to go home. This was the worst day of my life.

Joan was not my friend. She was too old. She was ten, and I was only seven. I had never spoken to her before because she was in the top class. She was all right, but she was just too old.

I wondered what Mum would say when she found out that I had lost Rosalyn. All that money – wasted. I knew she couldn't really afford it and I shouldn't have asked for one which was so expensive. Mum had bought the doll because she wanted me to be happy and I had lost it, and I certainly wasn't happy now.

I followed Mrs Wyant and Joan to Pebble Cottages, which were not far from the village hall, on the other side of the lane. There were five or six terraced cottages at right angles to the lane with long gardens running parallel to the lane. We turned into the gate on a cobbled path in front of the cottages.

Pebble Cottages

Mrs Wyant lived in the middle of the terrace. The front door opened on to a small living room. It was dark, like Peabody, not because there was a wall in front of the window, but because the window was too small. The cottage had a strange smell. I don't know what it was, but it didn't smell like home.

"I want to do a wee wee," I said. "The privy's at the bottom of the garden," replied Mrs Wyant.

"What do you mean – the privy?" I asked. I knew exactly what she meant.

"It's in the little black shed at the end of the path." I could not believe this - at the bottom of the garden and it was a very long garden!

"Just stay on our path. The other privies belong to the other cottages."

I started off on the forty-yard walk to the end of the garden. This was worse than Peabody. It's true that we didn't have our own toilet in our flat. It was outside on the landing and was shared by three families. We shared with Miss Farthing and Miss Phillips in No. 7, and the Jacklins in No. 9. Sometimes you had to wait, especially if it was Mr. Jacklin, who used to sit in there for a long time smoking his pipe. It was never very nice going in after him, but at least it wasn't very far to go and it wasn't out in the open. What would we do here if it was raining? We could get soaked, and it would be very cold in winter.

I opened the door of the little shed and there was a big black bucket with a wooden bench seat over it. The bucket was half full and the smell was strong and unpleasant. No wonder they didn't want it near the house.

I had no choice but to use it. When I had finished I started to put my hand up to pull the chain, out of habit, but I realised of course that there wasn't one. This was disgusting, and what would happen, I wondered, when the bucket was full?

I walked back slowly to the cottage. This was definitely the worst day of my life and I felt a lump in my throat as though I was going to cry. But sometimes when you are really unhappy, you don't cry, you just get very bad tempered and behave badly. And I knew how to behave badly. I criticised everything. I sulked and tried to be as uncooperative as possible.

Mrs Wyant had prepared a meal for us. I tried to eat it, but when you are nearly crying you do not feel hungry. I didn't try to explain why I couldn't eat it. I just pushed the plate away, saying, "This is horrible, I can't eat this. That's not what we have at home."

Poor Mrs Wyant ! If she had put her arm round me and said "What's the matter? Don't worry, I'll look after you," I would probably have burst into tears and told her how unhappy I felt, and that I was missing my Mum. She didn't know how to handle me, and I didn't really give her a chance.

My mouth was dry and I felt thirsty. "Can I have a drink of water, please?" I asked. She poured some water from a jug into a glass and handed it to me.

"Here you are," she said, hoping at last to please me.

"That's not clean," I complained. "You can't even see through it." It was cloudy and white like when you rinse out a milk bottle.

"Our water is always like that," she explained, "it comes from the well. It's only chalk and it won't hurt you."

"Well I don't want to drink chalk," I sulked.

"I'm sorry" said Mrs Wyant , "but that's all we have. All the houses in Radwell have chalky water. You'll just have to get used to it."

I was intrigued to know how you got chalky water from a well.

"The well is down by the gate where we came in," she said. "You'll see it soon when I fill the jugs."

The well was round, and made of bricks, with a tiled roof to stop too much dirt getting it. When you looked down, you couldn't see the bottom. There was just a white chalk wall as far as you could see. A big bucket was hanging on a hook just inside the well wall. It was attached to a long thick rope which was wound round the axle in the middle, "When we drop the bucket down the well, you have to keep out of the way of the handle because it goes round very fast on its own. It stops when the bucket hits the water and you then have to wait for the bucket to fill."

"How do you know when it's full?" "Well," she explained, "the bucket has to tip over and it sinks and fills up with water. You know it's full because it's heavy to wind it up again."

It was very heavy, and the hardest part was when the bucket reached the top, because you had to pull it to the edge of the well and tip the water into your own jugs.

"You're spilling it all!" I protested.

"You can't help spilling some," said Mrs Wyant, "and now you'll know not to waste any. And you see, the fresh water is still chalky."

"Well, at home, we always have clean water," was all I could think of to reply.

The day dragged on and it was beginning to get dark. I

just wished that Mum had not let me go on the coach. If she had
known how bad it was going to be, I'm sure she would have kept
me at home. She wouldn't have wanted me to be miserable and
unhappy like this. This was definitely the worst day of my life,
but still there were no tears. I don't think Joan liked it very much
either, but she didn't complain. She was polite and did as she was
told.

I continued to express my anger by finding new ways
of annoying Mrs Wyant. She had made up our beds for us and
she showed us where we were going to sleep. There were two
small camp beds, side by side, on what seemed like a small square
landing.

"This is not a bedroom. It's got stairs coming up in the
middle of it. You're not supposed to sleep on a landing."

Mrs Wyant was getting tired of arguing with me. "It's
getting late," she said, "When you've had a wash you can get
undressed and get into bed."

I was very tired and ready to sleep. I didn't think John
would be sleeping on a landing. I would go across the lane and
see him in the morning.

Joan and I talked for a little while, before settling down.
"Do you wish you were back in London with your Mum?" I asked.

"I haven't got a Mum, she died. Roy and I live with my
Dad."

I didn't know what to say. I couldn't imagine Mum dying,
and having to live without her.

"She was ill for a long time before she died," continued
Joan, "and I helped to look after her. She used to like it when I
brushed her hair. Now I have to help Dad look after Roy."

33

I began to feel a bit ashamed of the way I had been behaving. At least I would be able to go back to live with Mum when the war was over. I lay on the little bed thinking about Mum and Dad, and about the events of the day, until I began to feel sleepy. Then I heard Mrs Wyan coming up the stairs. If she had come five minutes later I would probably have been asleep.

I jumped out of bed and curled up in a small hard wooden chair, resting my head on the back of the chair, with my eyes shut.

"What are you doing on the chair?" she asked, obviously surprised.

"I'm trying to get to sleep," I replied, "and I think this will be more comfortable than that bed." I had scored another point.

"Well, it's time for lights out," she said, "you'd better get back into bed."

And at the same time that she was turning out the light, the whole country was being plunged into darkness. At sunset on September 1st 1939, the blackout began and it was to last for nearly six years.

Streetlamps were turned off, shop windows darkened and windows on all buildings – houses, offices, hospitals, stations, etc. – had to be covered with heavy blackout curtains so that not even a chink of light could be seen. If enemy aircraft were to fly overhead they would not be able to see towns and cities which would be a target for their bombs.

In the darkness of the room I eventually fell asleep on the bed, but not before I had tugged sheets, blankets and pillows into a crumpled heap on to the floor.

The next morning as soon as breakfast was over, Joan and I went across the lane to No. 2 Council Cottages. An elderly man with a very jolly face opened the door.

"We've come to see our brothers." I told him.

"Well, young ladies, you'd better come in. They're in the garden."

"What's your name?" I asked him.

"Me? I'm Uncle 'erbert." I liked the sound of that. I'd got quite a lot of uncles – about six, but I hadn't got an Uncle 'erbert.

"And what's her name?" I asked him.

"That's Auntie Edie". I liked them both. I noticed that he always called her 'Edie', because she wasn't his Auntie, but she never called him 'erbert'. She always called him 'Charles' or 'Charlie'. It didn't seem to matter – he was Uncle 'erbert to me.

He took us out into the garden. It was a square fenced garden with a gate at the bottom. John and Roy were playing ball with a black and white dog. I'd never had a dog, or any pet, and I was surprised to see how the dog seemed to understand the game. She would drop the ball in front of them and wait for someone to throw it for her, and then she would bring it back.

"What's the dog's name?" I asked.

"That's our Trixie," said Uncle 'erbert. The boys had now left the dog and were talking to Joan, and Trixie came over to Uncle 'erbert.

"She's a very clever dog, you know, she can even tell the time. She always tells me when it's seven o'clock. Don't you, Trixie?"

Trixie looked up lovingly at her master.

"Why does she tell you when it's seven o'clock?"

"Because that's when she has her chocolate buttons."

"Can I throw the ball for her?" I asked.

"Yes, of course you can. Throw it over that side on the grass, not near the fruit bushes, because some of them are prickly."

"Fruit bushes?" I asked.

"Yes," he explained, "we've got redcurrants, blackcurrants and gooseberries. They're nearly finished now. Auntie Edie makes pies and tarts with them and she has bottled some for the winter and made some jam."

I threw the ball for Trixie, she chased it and brought it back.

"You've got apples," I said, "and a lot of them have fallen on the grass."

"They're windfalls," explained Uncle 'erbert, "they might have maggots in them, but they'll be all right for cooking. Would you like an apple?" he asked.

"Oh, yes please."

"Well, let's pick you one from the tree." He stretched up to a high branch and pulled off an apple. "This looks a nice one," he said, and he polished it on his sleeve and gave it to me. "Here you are, young lady – a nice rosy apple for you." I remembered to say thank you.

".....and if you stay in Radwell very long, you will soon have nice rosy cheeks like the apple. I suppose you'd all like one now, wouldn't you?" he said to the others, and he gave them all an apple before he went back in.

"Do you like it here?" I asked John.

"Yes, it's all right here."

"Do you sleep on the landing?"

"Of course we don't, we sleep in a big bedroom."

"And where's your lav?" I asked, looking round for a small wooden shed.

"It's there, behind you, next to the back door."

I went to have a look. It wasn't in a wooden shed. It was part of the brick construction of the house, and was separated from it by a lobby. It had a bucket with a wooden seat, and the same funny smell, but at least you wouldn't get wet if it was raining.

"And do you have to get your water from a well?" I asked.

"No, there's a pump, come and have a look."

We went through the gate, and behind the gardens of the next two cottages. The pump provided water for the six council cottages. There was a big iron handle which had to be pumped up and down. For the first three or four pumps nothing seemed to happen, then the water came gushing out. It was much easier than the well, but I couldn't see if it was clear.

"Does it look clean when you drink it, or is it chalky?"

"It's chalky, but it tastes all right," said John.

He and Roy seemed to have struck lucky. It was true that they had a smelly bucket and cloudy water, but they didn't have to go down to the bottom of the garden, and the pump seemed far superior to the well because dirt couldn't fall down it, and it wasn't so dangerous. They didn't have to sleep on a landing, and they had Uncle 'erbert and Auntie Edie. If I couldn't be with Mum and Dad, I wanted to be here.

I had a plan and I needed Joan's cooperation.

"I've been thinking," I said to Joan when we were back across the lane, "It seems to be much better over in the Council Cottages, and I've had an idea. If I say that my Mum and Dad said I've got to be with my brother, and you say that your Dad wants you to look after Roy, they might let us change over. You might be able to go over to the Council Cottages with Roy, and John could come with me."

Joan seemed to think this was a good idea and agreed to go along with the plan. The change would be quite simple.

Then I became a Jekyll and Hyde character, friendly and polite, charming and helpful whenever I was with Uncle 'erbert and Auntie Edie; sullen and uncooperative with poor old Mrs Wyant. I knew that if anyone was going to cross the lane, it wouldn't be Joan.

Later that day Mr Payne came down the lane. He had been billeted with Mr Cross at the top of the lane, on the corner of the Stotfold road. We ran up the lane to meet him.

"How are you all getting on," he asked, "have you settled down nicely?"

"I'm supposed to be with my brother," I said. "My Mum and Dad said we were to stay together. We're not supposed to be in different houses, and Joan's supposed to be with her brother, aren't you, Joan?"

"Yes," said Joan, "my Dad said I've got to look after Roy."

"Oh," said Mr Payne, "we'll have to see."

It was obvious that someone had decided to split the two families in this way to have the same sex evacuees sharing a room, but it would be all right sharing a bedroom with a boy, if he was your brother.

"I always sleep in the same bedroom as John, when we are at home," I told Auntie Edie, "we are used to being in the same room."

I continued with my Jekyll and Hyde behaviour for the rest of the day, getting rather impatient that it seemed to be taking so long.

THE DECLARATION OF WAR

Next morning, Sunday September 3rd, Mr Payne came down the lane again carrying a bag. "June and Roy," he said, "I want both of you to go and collect all your things together and change places. We think it will be better if brothers and sisters are billeted together. So June, you can go and stay with Mr and Mrs Edwards. Oh, and by the way, is this your doll?" Out of the bag came Rosalyn.

"Oh yes, that's Rosalyn. She's mine. Look, she shuts her eyes," I said, tipping her backwards, hoping that my knowledge of her special talent would be proof of ownership.

I ran back over the cobblestones to the cottage to collect my belongings. "I've been told I've got to get my things and move across the road," I said, trying to sound bewildered and surprised. This was nothing to do with me. I was just doing as I was told. Joan was standing there but I could not look her in the eye. She knew how devious I had been. I had got my own way and would not have to spend a third night with Mrs Wyant.

At 11.15am, there was a message on the wireless from the Prime Minister:

> "I am speaking to you from the Cabinet room at 10, Downing Street. This morning the British Ambassador in Berlin handed the German government the final note stating that unless we heard from them, by 11 o'clock, that they were prepared, at once, to withdraw their troops

from Poland a state of war would exist between us.

I have to tell you now that no such undertaking has been received and that consequently this country is at war with Germany."

Neville Chamberlain   September 3rd 1939 11.15am

There was an air of gloom everywhere. We were at war. How was this going to affect our lives? All around was a sense of anxiety and uncertainty, but I was happy: I had got my own way; I had got Rosalyn back; and we were going to live in the Council Cottages with Auntie Edie, Uncle 'erbert and Trixie.

* * * * * * * * *

PART THREE

'Radwell 1939 to 1943'

'...childhood moving like a sigh through the green woods ...'
W H Auden. New Year's Letter 1941

My intuition had proved to be reliable. I had had the strong feeling that going to live with Auntie Edie and Uncle 'erbert would be a good move and it was the beginning of a long, happy and loving relationship. Auntie Edie had chosen John and Roy because she was used to boys. She and Uncle 'erbert had two sons of their own, now grown up and living away, and they had never had a girl. I was to stay with them throughout my primary school years until I was eleven years old.

There were never any arguments, and they were never angry. They liked me and I was happy, and because I was happy, I was good. They never saw the unfriendly, uncooperative little girl that Mrs Wyant had to contend with. I was the daughter that they never had.

I missed Mum and Dad, of course, but like the other evacuees and the foster parents, I accepted evacuation as necessary and knew we had to make the best of it. And of all the foster parents, I was sure that Auntie Edie and Uncle 'erbert were the best.

They seemed to be very old, like Grandma, or even older.

Auntie Edie was a big lady who moved very slowly, and she wore her long grey hair wound round in a bun. When she laughed you could see that some of her teeth were missing and those that were left looked long and loose. In later years I realised that they were both over sixty when I arrived. They were very kind people.

No consideration was given as to the suitability of the foster parents to look after children. Age was no barrier and some evacuees, like us, were billeted with elderly couples. Inevitably, some placements were totally unsuitable and many children were neglected, exploited or abused. Teenage boys, for example, were seen as a lucrative replacement for farmworkers who had been called up for National Service. At that time an average pay packet for a labourer was £3 a week, and evacuees could work for nothing. At busy times, like harvesting, they were kept away from school on the pretext of being ill, and many had their education seriously disrupted.

A girl I knew, whom I will not name for obvious reasons, confided in me many years later that she had been sexually abused regularly for two years from the age of nine.

It has been estimated that one in eight evacuees suffered in some way.

No welfare visits were made after the evacuation to see if the children had settled in happily and no consideration given to the psychological stress which was probably felt by all evacuees. Understandably, many had problems which resulted in difficult behaviour or bedwetting. The government seemed to be unwilling or unable to help in any way, although the 'Women's Voluntary Service for Civil Defence' (W.V.S.) published a leaflet:

John and I did not experience any problems in settling down in our new environment. We were to share a big bedroom with two beds. John had the big double bed in the alcove and I was to sleep in the camp bed facing the window. The room was at the front of the house facing Pebble Cottages. I would be able to see Mrs Wyant, and Joan and Roy when they took the long walk to their privy, but they wouldn't be able to see me.

I put all my clothes in the drawer and sat Rosalyn on the bed. It was a plain room with lino on the floor and no colour on the walls. It was much bigger than our bedroom at home, and I liked it. There was a washstand with a big bowl and a jug of water. There was a soap dish and a towel and I would be able to wash myself in the morning when I got up before going downstairs. And there was a po under the bed.

"Come downstairs now June," Auntie Edie called, "Your teacher's here."

"Are you all right now?" asked Mr Payne.

"Yes, I like it here, and I'm glad I've got Rosalyn back. She was new and she cost a lot of money."

Mr Payne had been down the lane to see all the evacuees. He had to give us the official postcard to fill in.

"You don't really need one, do you, because your address is the same as John's, so you could put your name on his card."

"No, I want my own card," I insisted, and he gave one to me. It was the 'Official Postcard' to tell our parents where we were.

"What does c/o mean?" I asked.

"That stands for 'care of'' and you have to put c/o Mr and Mrs C Edwards."

Auntie Edie wrote down the address and I had to copy it carefully.

2 Council Cottages,

Radwell

Nr Baldock,

Herts

OFFICIAL POSTCARD

From _____

C/o _____

_____

_____

This is my new address.
Please address letters correctly as shown above

At the bottom I wrote 'I like it here'. Mr Payne collected all the cards and checked to make sure they were correct.

"Your parents will soon know where you are and I expect they'll write to you."

"Will they be able to come and see us as well?" I asked.

"Yes, in a little while, I expect they will be able to visit you."

That would be good. I would be able to show them my room and the garden, and they would be able to see Auntie Edie and Uncle 'erbert and Trixie. I wouldn't tell them about my two nights with Mrs Wyant, nor about losing Rosalyn. There are some things that are best forgotten.

* * * * * * * * * *

Auntie Edie had been peeling the potatoes for dinner. She put the potatoes in a bowl and covered them with water. Then she put the potato peelings into a big black saucepan and put it on the stove.

"My mum always throws the potato peelings away." I said, looking in the saucepan. They didn't look very clean and I wondered if we would have to eat them.

"Oh, they're not for us," said Auntie Edie, "they're for the chickens."

"What chickens?"

"We keep chickens at the top of the garden. You'll see them later."

"The peelings are very dirty." I said, "Don't they mind the dirt?"

"No, they don't mind," she said, "They have to eat a lot of grit for the eggshells."

"Eggshells?" I was getting even more confused.

"In the laying season they lay eggs every day. You'll be able to have one for breakfast in the morning."

When the peelings were cooked, Auntie Edie drained them and put them into a big bowl. While they were still hot, she sprinkled some brown powder over them.

"What's that?"

"It's bran. We stir in the bran so that all the peelings are coated with it."

It smelled wonderful. I was beginning to feel hungry and it wouldn't have taken much to have persuaded me to eat some.

"The chicken's food is ready, Charlie." Said Auntie Edie, and Uncle 'erbert picked up the bowl. "Come on, you two," he said, "let's go and feed the chickens and collect the eggs. Here you are, you can carry the bowl." We went through the gate to a long unfenced garden.

"Is this your garden as well?"

"Yes," said Uncle 'erbert, "This is where we grow our vegetables. That's where I dug up the potatoes and carrots for dinner." There were peas and tomatoes climbing up sticks. There were runner beans on tall frames with netting, and big fat marrows lying on the ground. It was like a greengrocer's shop. You wouldn't have to buy anything. Free vegetables - and now we were going to get free eggs as well.

The chicken run was at the top of the garden, surrounded by high wire netting, to keep the foxes out. The chickens ran towards us noisily, waiting to be fed. Uncle 'erbert opened the gate and went in. He tipped the food into a long trough and the hens rushed to get it. If it tasted as good as it smelled, it must have been delicious.

While the hens were eating, we went into the hen-house. There were nesting boxes lined with straw, with eggs in them.

"Put all the eggs in the bowl," said Uncle 'erbert.

I didn't like the smell in the henhouse and the eggs didn't really look very nice. They were dirty. They had sticky chicken droppings all over them and bits of straw stuck on.

In London we always had clean eggs. "They're very dirty," I said to Uncle 'erbert, and I hoped they would still taste nice.

"Oh, that's nothing," he replied, "It'll wash off. It won't look like that when it's in your egg cup."

There was a bowl full of eggs – and they were all free.

I remembered a bowl full of eggs we had at home. Mum had been shopping and had put the eggs in a bowl on the table. Basil, the baby, was just big enough to reach up and pull the bowl on to the floor. Mum came running, but she was too late. All the eggs were broken. It was a disaster.

"It wasn't his fault," said Mum, "I shouldn't have left the bowl so near the edge of the table." She wasn't cross with the baby, but she was clearly upset. John burst into tears, so I cried too.

"Don't cry," she said, "it couldn't be helped. It was an accident." But John was inconsolable. The more he cried, the more I realised that this was a major catastrophe. Mum had very little money to spend on food, and she had to plan our meals very carefully. She cleared up the mess and the incident would probably have been forgotten had it not been for John worrying about it for the rest of the day. He would suddenly burst into tears, just saying 'All those eggs!' Each time, Mum tried to comfort him and reassure him that it would be all right, but still, at intervals, he would cry again, saying 'All those eggs'. I realised, for the first time in my life, that we were poor.

Now, here I was picking up free eggs. Well – nearly free. Auntie Edie had to buy the bran, but the potato peelings were free. Life in Radwell was going to be quite different from life at home. Mum would like it, I was sure, and she wouldn't have to worry about broken eggs; but I wasn't so sure about Dad. I didn't think he would be able to dig the garden and do all the work and he wouldn't like digging a big hole to empty the bucket. Dad didn't really like doing things. He liked to sit in his chair and read the 'Greyhound Express'.

I remembered one occasion when I was about 6 years old, coming home from school very hungry. Mummy was out, but Daddy was always at home because he didn't have a job.

"Daddy, I'm starving hungry," I said, "Can I have a jam sandwich?"

"Mammy won't be long," he replied, "She'll be home presently," and he stayed in the chair, reading his newspaper.

By the time Mum came home, I was ravenous. "Can I have a jam sandwich, please, I'm starving," I said as she opened the door.

"Oh give me a chance to get inside the door," she replied wearily. She was laden with heavy shopping bags and had already worked at two of her jobs. She went out early every morning, while we were still in bed, to do her office cleaning. She came home to get us up and ready for school, and then went to her second job. In the evening, she went out again to work as a waitress.

Dad did nothing in the house to help her, not even the washing-up, and Mum didn't really expect him to. It was humiliating and soul-destroying for Dad to be unemployed for so many years. It would have been the final degradation if he were expected to do the woman's work, and it was the same in many families. Some men, of course, wanted to ease the burden, which fell on their wives. I heard of one man, home all day on his own, who used to draw the curtains so that he could clean the house without being seen by his neighbours.

It was widely recognised that women had to work until they were ready to drop if they were to earn enough from their low-paid jobs to support the family. Schools helped by taking children into the infants from the age of three and the miserable plight of women was expressed in the popular song of the 'thirties 'Try a Little Tenderness':

> *She may be weary,*
> *Women do get weary*
> *Wearing that old shabby dress.*

When she is weary,
Try a little tenderness.

You know she's waiting,
Just anticipating
Things she may never possess.
While she is waiting,
Try a little tenderness.

It's not just sentimental,
She has her grief and her care,
And the soft words that are spoken,
Make it easier to bear.

You won't regret it,
Women don't forget it,
Love is her one happiness.
And it's so easy,
Try a little tenderness.

I never saw Dad show her any tenderness. He never put his arm round her to show any love or appreciation. She used to wait on him hand and foot, like a servant, and she never complained. She was a saint and she deserved a better life.

Now she was waiting to be evacuated, because she had the baby. I wondered where she would go. I hoped she would be sent to somewhere like Radwell with fields and trees, and a big garden, with fresh fruit and vegetables and free eggs. Perhaps she would be lucky and live with some kind people like Uncle 'erbert and Auntie Edie where she would be appreciated, and could be happy. She deserved a little happiness.

* * * * * * * * *

Life at No. 2 Council Cottages was very good right from the start. Uncle 'erbert was funny, and he was always joking or teasing. Auntie Edie looked after everybody and cooked lovely meals. With fresh homegrown fruit and vegetables always available, we had plenty to eat, even when food was rationed. No doubt the chickens provided a valuable source of meat, although this never occurred to me at any time, and there was never any hint that a bird had been killed. I imagine that this was done discreetly so that I would not be upset.

During the week, we had our dinner in the evening at half past six when Uncle 'erbert came home. He worked at Simpsons' Brewery in Baldock.

Trixie, the dog, would sit and watch us, occasionally receiving titbits from the table. As soon as we had finished she would jump on the fireside chair, putting her front paws on the back of the chair with her nose pointing towards the cupboard.

"There you are, you see," said Uncle 'erbert, "she's telling me that it's seven o'clock and time for her chocolate buttons, aren't you, Trixie?"

She would stay there, wagging her tail, and woofing quietly until Uncle 'erbert gave her the daily allowance. Even when sweets were rationed they always made sure that Trixie had her chocolate buttons.

I looked at the clock and he was right. It was seven o'clock but it was quite a while before I realised that it was the end of our meal that was the signal for Trixie to jump on the chair.

* * * * * * * * * *

Of all the places to which evacuees were being sent, I think it would have been difficult to find a place more different

50

from Herbrand Street, than Radwell. The tall grey claustrophobic brick walls and concrete had given way to green fields, open spaces and the sky. Where there was noisy traffic and smoke-filled air, here there was peace and stillness, the scent of wild flowers and the smell of animals. Herbrand Street and Peabody Buildings were so crowded that most of the people you saw were strangers, but you would not be able to live in Radwell for long without getting to know the entire population of 40 to 50 people living in the eighteen houses. There was Radwellbury Farm and a very pretty little church dating back to the fourteenth century, with beautiful stained-glass windows, but there were no shops. The nearest shops were in Baldock, two miles away down the Great North Road, or in Stotfold, across the fields.

Down the hill past the church was Radwell House which was originally the Manor House. It was always known to us as The White House because the stables, which were adjacent to the lane, were painted white. The house had been requisitioned by the government for use as an army base, for a regiment of the Royal Signals. If you looked past the sentry on duty at the gate to the square beyond, you could see young recruits on parade being shouted at by their superiors as they learned to march in time. They would hoist their rifles up on their shoulders and back down again. They were being prepared for war.

Not far past the White House was the old stone bridge crossing the river Ivel, with a magnificent view of the Mill House across the lake.

That was where Mrs de Zoote lived and was now the home of Pat Middlemass. Even Pat, who had been to a private school, could not have had a view like this

The Mill House

from her bedroom window in London. The bridge was really the end of the lane. You could bear left and follow a track through the woods to Webb's Meadows, or take the right fork to the Mill House. There was a board saying:

PRIVATE ROAD – NO THOROUGHFARE
Trespassers will be
prosecuted

We were allowed to go along the road only with special permission. I recall going past that board once when I went to see Ruth Prater, who was billeted on the Mill House Estate, and on Sundays when we went to the Mill House for Sunday School. Other than that, it was strictly out of bounds. We were all very law-abiding, and I knew my place.

That was Radwell. Go for a five minute walk and you'd seen it all – except, of course, for miles of footpaths which went through woods where you could gather nuts, and across meadows where you could make daisy chains; you could paddle in brooks with tiddlers waiting to be caught in jam jars, and frogspawn which slipped through your fingers; you could watch a butterfly fly away as you released it from your gently cupped hands; and you could make a grasshopper jump by tickling its long back legs with a blade of grass. Now, that was Radwell!

NEWNHAM SCHOOL

There was always somewhere to go and something to do, different games to play, and things to discover and lessons to be learned. But there was no school.

"There's no school here, Auntie Edie," I said, after I had explored the village. "Don't we have to go to school anymore?"

"The school's in Newnham," she replied, "and you'll be starting in a few days." Newnham was the next village on the other side of the Great North Road, about a mile and a half away. "There's a school bus," she said, "it comes up the Stotfold lane and you'll have to be on the corner by 8 o'clock."

This was going to be another adventure and off we went with our packed lunches and our gasmasks. Our green school bus, marked 'PRIVATE', snaked its way along the narrow winding country lane to Newnham, where it stopped at the village green.

"Seniors, stay on the bus please," said Mr Payne, "we're going on to Ashwell. The rest of you get off now. You're going with Miss Reddall."

Miss Reddall was waiting for us at the bus stop. The two teachers exchanged a few words as we were handed over to her charge and more seniors got on the bus to go to the Secondary School.

We followed Miss Reddall a short distance across the green to her village school. It didn't look like a school. It wasn't big enough, although it did have a school bell on top of the roof. There were no corridors or stairs, and no big hall with a platform, just a lobby to hang our coats, and two classrooms. All the infants went through to Mrs Peacock's room and we older children stayed in the first classroom. We had one room for all the juniors, aged 7 years to 11 years, with one teacher. It was four classes in one. This was my first year in junior school but I hadn't expected to be in the same class as John, who was in the top class.

Miss Reddall sorted us out. She already had our names on a register, and gave us our places. She was a really nice teacher. She was very friendly and made us all feel welcome, but she was strict. We knew that she always expected us to do as we were told – and we did. Lessons were quite different from Christ Church, but at home I had only been in the infants, so it would have been different anyway.

Once you got used to it, it was very good. Sometimes she gave us different things to do according to our age, like easier sums or spellings to learn, but quite often we all worked together. It didn't really matter how old you were, nor which class you were supposed to be in. If you could do something, you did it, and if you couldn't, Miss Reddall helped you.

It must have been quite difficult for Miss Reddall, because as well as teaching four classes at once, which she was used to doing, the school had more than doubled in size. There were more evacuees than local children, and it was a bit crowded. But when there's a war, everyone has to put up with it.

Soon after morning school started the milkman arrived delivering our bottles of milk for playtime.

"It's going to be a few extra bottles today, isn't it?" he said, as he looked at the crowded classroom. Miss Reddall agreed laughing, "Yes, and I think they are going to keep me busy."

We drank our milk at playtime, one third of a pint in small bottles made especially for the schools. Sometimes, if you were lucky, there were a few over and you could have two.

The school playground was alongside the classrooms and on the far side were the toilets, backing on to the meadow behind. I was not expecting flush toilets, but here, there were not even buckets. There were wooden bench seats with holes in them and below, a sloping concrete floor so that everything could slide away. The boys' toilets were next to ours and we could hear them above the dividing partition. Sometimes they were very rude. They would look to see if something was stuck on the way down, and then they would take it in turns to use the same cubicle so that they could aim at it, and watch it slide to the bottom. You could hear them cheer when they got it on the move.

The back wall of the toilets was open at the bottom so that you could see everything floating into the meadow behind. At dinnertime, we were allowed to go and play in the meadow, and the area behind the school was fenced off. If your ball went over the fence, it was lost forever, floating in the bog. We never played near there as we did not like the smell and there were too many flies. It would not have been a good idea to have buckets because with so many of us, they would need emptying everyday, and you couldn't expect Miss Reddall to do that.

She lived in the School House which was next to the school, and there was a door in the corner of our classroom leading into her house. She had her own toilet, but Mrs Peacock, the infants' teacher had to use ours. She came from Royston and used to travel to school on a motorbike. She was usually dressed in leather, with a black leather hat strapped under her chin like a pilot.

I don't think Mrs Peacock liked me. One day, when it was raining, we had to stay in at playtime and dinnertime, and we were allowed to go into the infants' room. There was a magnificent rocking horse in there which I liked to ride on. I made it go forwards and backwards as high as it would go, which made it clonk at each end.

"Don't do that," she said, "you'll break it."

Well, I didn't want to break it, but you didn't know how far it would go until it clonked.

That may have been why she didn't like me, or it might have been what happened in the toilets. I was in the middle toilet, talking to my friend across the dividing partition.

"Do you still bite your nails?" I asked.

"Yes, do you?"

"Yes," I called back, and then, as an afterthought, "and I bite my toenails as well."

As I came out of the cubicle, Mrs Peacock emerged from the end one.

"You're a very dirty little girl," was all she said, as she walked off in disgust. I'd never thought it was dirty, and it seemed the easiest way to get your toenails off when they got too long and started to press against your shoes.

It never occurred to me to ask Auntie Edie to cut them for me and she didn't seem to think of it. I was learning to be very independent, and to solve my own problems, which you have to do when there's a war on.

* * * * * * * * *

The 'Official Postcard' giving our new address had arrived in London. Mum and Dad were relieved to know that we had arrived safely and Mum wrote us a letter.

"They're coming to see us!" we shouted, "They're coming next Sunday."

In general, travelling was discouraged as buses and trains were needed to move people on essential war work. There were posters at stations and bus-stops asking:

'IS YOUR JOURNEY REALLY NECESSARY?'

However, 'Special Travel Facilities' were available to parents at a low price for visits to evacuated children.

> "......special cheap rail facilities will be available for visits to children …..
> The general aim will be to provide special train facilities on Sundays at monthly intervals to reception areas. The return fare will be at the rate of the ordinary single fare.

> Minister of Transport
> House of Commons
> 15th November 1939

Mum and Dad had applied for the vouchers to buy these tickets, and were given instructions on how to get to us. It was very exciting.

I was sure that they would like Uncle 'erbert, who was very funny, and Auntie Edie, who would cook them a nice dinner. I was glad that they would not have to meet Mrs Wyant. If I had still been across the lane with her, I think I would have cried and pleaded with them to take me home with them.

Instead, it was a wonderful reunion with lots of hugs and kisses, and they were obviously relieved to see that we were happy and well looked after. Dad was not entirely impressed. Once, when he was looking at me, he said to Mum, very quietly "Just look at her hair!" I don't know what was wrong with my hair but obviously he didn't like it.

We showed Mum and Dad our bedroom, with Rosalyn asleep on my pillow. Then we took them up the garden to see the chickens and collect the eggs. I explained how they were fed on potato peelings and bran, and that we had fresh eggs for breakfast.

We showed them our dugout. This was our air-raid shelter halfway up the garden. Everyone had been advised to prepare a safe place for members of their family, giving protection from enemy bombing if it occurred. There were many different kinds of shelter. Some houses had a 'Morrison Shelter' which was like a steel table surrounded by wire. Some families converted a cellar or a cupboard under the stairs, using sandbags to reinforce the area. Where space was available in built-up areas, public shelters were built, with steel bunk beds and chemical toilets. Our dugout was a simplified version of an 'Anderson Shelter'. It was a large hole in the ground covered with corrugated iron. There were steps on one side to get down into it, and once inside there was a wide ledge with enough room for four or five people to sit down. This was Uncle 'erbert's work, and like the well across the lane, the walls were hard white chalk.It was very re-assuring to know that we had a place of safety to go to in an emergency even though Radwell had been designated as a 'safe area'. We all hoped we would never have to use it.

Mum and Dad could see we were in safe hands. After dinner we went for a walk and we showed them the farm, the church, the White House, and the Mill House across the lake.

Then it was time for them to leave. There was only one bus to Baldock in the afternoon at five o'clock and they had to catch their train. We walked with them up to the bus stop. I was sad that they had to go but I was pleased that they had seen my new home. I liked it here very much and was happy, but as the bus came into view, I nearly started to cry. I wanted them to stay or to take me with them. They kissed us goodbye, and I could feel tears coming into my eyes. We stood and waved until the bus was out of sight, and then walked slowly back to the house without speaking. I wanted the war to end so that I could go home again and live with Mum and Dad.

RADWELLBURY FARM

Radwellbury Farm was the centre of village life. The farmhouse was a big impressive building and Mr Walker, the farmer, always looked very important. He usually wore a tweed jacket and clean shoes and you hardly ever saw him near the muck in the cowsheds.

It was Mr Wyant, the foreman, who did all the dirty work. He lived with his family in the old cottage next to the farm. The population of Radwell was very small, and there were few children of school age in the village so his ten-year-old daughter Joan was delighted when Jean Hanwell and Doris Van der Wheel were billeted at the farm.

Joan's mother, also Mrs Wyant, was sister-in-law to Mrs Wyant in Pebble Cottages, but I never saw them together.

When Joan's mother was out, we used to go and play

with Joan. It was wonderful. The cottage was rambling and mysterious, the most exciting place I could imagine. It was dark with stone floors and low ceilings. There was a big fireplace in a large chimney-breast, and there were nooks and crannies, corridors and stairs. There was a passageway which went through to the scullery and the dairy, with a back door opening on to the farmyard, with milking sheds.

From the living room we could go along a corridor to the drawing room where there was a piano. In the corner of this room was a flight of stairs leading to the bedrooms. In the top corridor, we could go past the bedrooms into the lumber-room, which was used for storage. In the autumn, apples were spread out on the wooden floor with spaces between them so that if one should start to rot, it would not spread to the others. To this day, I can't smell apples or cider without being transported back to that room. There was a big tin chest in the room filled with dressing-up clothes and we spent many wet days up there, living in a world of fantasy. There were more stairs in the corner of the lumber-room with a door at the bottom, which brought us back to where we started.

Joan was very attractive and quite talented. She could play the piano and I watched with incredulous admiration as she played a tune called 'Eighteenth Century Drawing Room'. It was years before I identified the piece as part of Mozart's piano sonata in 'C'. When I hear it played today the words that we used to sing still come to mind and I am back in that old farm cottage watching Joan's fingers tapping the keys on the drawing room piano.

I looked up to Joan as a role model. Certainly, if we'd had a May Day Festival, there would have been no question of who would have been Queen of the May.

Joan had a lovely voice and was in the church choir, and

as she was my role model, I joined the choir as well. Mr Turner, the organist and choirmaster gave me a voice test and told me that I was a soprano. I loved singing and had a good ear for music and had no difficulty in reaching the top notes. The best part of being in the choir was wearing the beautiful robes. John was not so lucky as the boys wore long black cassocks under a short white surplus, but the girls wore deep purple. Our robes were very long and pleated with enormous sleeves, like an academic gown, with a matching soft four-cornered hat. I hoped I looked as good as Joan who looked absolutely magnificent in her gown. Not surprisingly, John fell in love with her.

I used to tease him, "I know who you love," I taunted, but he ignored me. "You love Joan Wyant, don't you?"

"Shut up," he replied.

Sixty years later I explored the subject again. "Do you remember Joan Wyant?" I asked John.

"Remember her? Of course I do. I was in love with her."

"I knew you were. I said so at the time."

"Well, what you didn't know," he continued, "was that I went to her house and knocked at the door. Her mother answered the door and I asked her if I could take Joan to the pictures. She said 'No' – and that was the end of that love affair."

Joan now looks back over the years, and says, "I was in love with him, too." And when told about her mother's uncooperative response, she said, "Oh, I didn't know that and I wondered why our romance came to such a sudden end."

The course of true love never did run smooth – not even for a 'Queen'.

CHRISTMAS

The first few months of the war passed quietly. The enemy attacks which had been anticipated had not happened and the 'Phoney War', as it was called, led to a sense of complacency and false security. With Christmas approaching and families wanting to be together, many evacuees drifted home. Mum knew that John and I had settled down happily with Auntie Edie and Uncle 'erbert, and that we were both doing well at school, and a return to London for us was not considered. In many ways we were much better off.

Although I was happy in my billet, it seemed very unfair that we would not have a proper Christmas at home, hanging up our pillowcase at the bottom of the bed to be filled with toys and sweets from Santa Claus. I was not sure how it would work out in Radwell. We would miss Mum's Christmas dinner. She was a good cook and we would have had turkey or chicken. Grandma always came to dinner, and sometimes Dad's brother, Uncle Monty. Dad did the carving and we all wanted a leg which was the best part, so Dad always made sure that we all had one. We must have had the only six-legged turkey in the market.

Then there was Mum's Christmas pudding. She used to put silver threepenny bits in the mixture and you were very lucky if you got one – and yet we seemed to get one every time.

Christmas would not be the same in Radwell. The local children were lucky. The war wouldn't really make any difference to them, but it was a sad time for us.

The government did not want the evacuees to go home for Christmas, as they feared that many would not return afterwards to the safe areas. Although there had been no enemy attacks so far, they believed that the threat was real and they wanted the children to stay away from the cities. Directives were issued, asking billeting officers to organise events and activities in the safe areas to persuade us to stay. The ladies in the villages responded and decided to do something about it.

The word went round. 'There's going to be a party for the evacuees'. It was going to be held in the village hall in Newnham on the Saturday before Christmas. Newnham was bigger than Radwell and there were more evacuees there. Those of us from the smaller, outlying villages would be taken in on the school bus. It was all very exciting and it would go a long way to make up for our deprivation. It made us feel very special and important.

"We're having a party!" I said to some of my classmates, hoping to make them envious. "You won't be able to come, it's just for the evacuees."

The big day came. Off I went wearing my best dress, and with new ribbons in my hair. The village hall had been transformed. There was a Christmas tree and the hall was decorated with coloured paper chains and tinsel, and balloons were hanging from the ceiling.

Food was beginning to be in short supply and there had been warnings that rationing was soon to begin, but there was no sign of shortages here. The ladies had excelled themselves. They had made tablecloths out of red crepe paper and they were spread with food. There were plates of sandwiches, cakes with currants in, cakes with icing on. There was red jelly, pink blancmange and jugs of lemonade and orange juice - everything for a wonderful party.

We were going to play games like musical chairs, squeak piggy squeak, and pinning the tail on the donkey. There were prizes to be won – and there was going to be a Father Christmas after tea. There was everything here for a wonderful party. But best of all, were the faces of the local children crowding in the doorway, trying to get a glimpse of the excitement. I skipped round the hall, doing extra high skips as I went past the door, showing off, so that they could see how much I was enjoying myself. They started to edge forward to get a better view, making an envious crowd in the corner of the hall – but this was our party. We were going to enjoy ourselves and they could see we were enjoying ourselves. And they could only stand and watch.

I don't know whose idea it was, but somebody felt sorry for them, and decided that there would be enough food for them as well.

"Come on in, then," someone said, "you might as well join in. We'll have a bigger party. I'm sure there is enough food for all of you."

And in they came – running, and shrieking with delight. It just wasn't fair. This was supposed to have been an evacuees' party. They would be able to have a proper Christmas with their family, and we were going to have this party instead. Now they would be having both. The exhilaration I had been feeling disappeared, completely destroyed by the unfairness of it all. If they had said it was going to be a children's party for everyone, that would have been different, but that was not what they had said. It was supposed to be an evacuees' party, and it wasn't. And now it was a big disappointment.

I was glad to get back home.

"Hello," said Auntie Edie, "Did you enjoy yourself?"

"No, not really," I replied, "someone let all the Newnham children in, and that spoilt it."

"Oh, you mustn't talk like that," said Auntie Edie, "that's very selfish."

Auntie Edie didn't understand, and I realised that she was disappointed in me. This made me feel even worse. Auntie Edie was a very kind and loving person, and I wanted to please her. This was one of only two occasions in four years that I can recall, when she was not pleased with me.

* * * * * * * * *

The following day was Sunday and there was a Carol Service at the church in the afternoon. It was getting dark and the church look mysterious by candlelight. There was a crib with the Holy Family in the manger surrounded by the animals, and we listened to the Christmas story and sang all the favourite carols. When we sang 'Away in a Manger', all the children gathered round the crib to sing on their own. We prayed for peace on earth and goodwill towards men. Christmas in Radwell seemed to be very special.

During the week that followed, we went carol singing. We wrapped up warmly and sang outside all the houses. We were carrying lanterns and candles in jam jars, and we ended up at the Mill House. Mrs de Zoote invited us in and we sang our carols in the big hall. Then we went and stood round the fire in the kitchen to have mince pies and hot cocoa.

I was enjoying Christmas, although I was already beginning to have doubts about Santa Claus. I wanted to believe in him, but the other children were probably right when they said that he wasn't real. And if there was a Santa Claus, he probably wouldn't be able to get round when there was a war on, so we weren't really expecting any presents. I did not know that Mum had sent a parcel to Auntie Edie, and on Christmas morning she gave us our presents. I had a new jumper, some crayons and a puzzle book, and 'Black Beauty' by Anna Sewell. It was a lovely surprise, and although I missed Mum and Dad, and Baby Basil, I was really enjoying my first Christmas away from home. There was magic in the air in Radwell.

FOOD RATIONING

Christmas passed and the New Year began. We all hoped that 1940 would bring peace, and that we would be able to go home, but the signs were not encouraging and January was hard. We had been issued with ration books before the outbreak of war but had been hoping that we would never have to use them.

On January 15th, food rationing began. Butter, meat and fresh eggs were among the first foods to be rationed, and people were encouraged to buy margarine, corned beef and dried egg powder. Stocks of food in the country were getting low and Merchant Navy ships carrying essential imports were finding it difficult to get through enemy lines. The British Navy, which escorted the supply ships, could not always detect the enemy submarines which were lurking in the deep waters of the shipping lanes. A direct torpedo attack from below could sink a ship, with a tragic loss of life and all the essential food supplies. Food production at home had also dropped, as many young men had been recruited into the armed services from the factories and farms. Their places were filled from the vast numbers of previously unemployed who were now an essential workforce.

Gone were the days when able-bodied men languished in the dole queues, and rotted on the scrap heap of society, their talents unrecognised and not required. Now, everybody was needed. Those young enough to fight were drafted into the armed services, and the rest had to fill the gaps left by the servicemen.

Dad was too old to be called up. He was forty-five when war was declared, fifteen years older than Mum, and he went into the Civil Service. His grade was never more than 'temporary' although he always clung to the hope that he would be put on to the permanent pensionable staff after the war. At least now he had a job. For him, and many like him, the war was his salvation.

This new workforce might have been grateful for the opportunity to earn a living, but they were out of the practice of working, and were often totally inexperienced in their new jobs. It would take time to organise and train them so that they could be really productive. The dwindling food stocks and the difficulty in getting regular supplies from abroad made rationing inevitable.

Each month, the value of a coupon would be announced, and this would vary from month to month depending on the availability of each commodity. The weekly butter allowance, for example, might go down from three ounces per person, to two ounces.

We were encouraged to have two thick slices of bread, instead of three thin ones, and as the slices got smaller towards the end of the loaf, we were told to spread our butter on the small side, so that we could spread it to the edge.

Food rationing was not the only hardship to be faced in

January. It was cold. Radwell was much colder than London, with no tall buildings to provide shelter from the bitter east wind. There was no central heating in the houses and coal was also in short supply. When the fire went out in the hearth at the end of the day, Jack Frost would freeze everything in his icy grip. When you woke in the morning there were icicles on the windows and the condensation on the glass formed a thick layer of ice.

Miss Reddall always seized upon an opportunity to link her lessons to our experiences, and at the first heavy frost of the winter, we learned a poem called '*THE FROST*', and one of the verses was as follows:

He came to the windows of those who slept
And over each pane like a fairy crept
Wherever he breathed, wherever he stepped
  By the light of the moon were seen
Most beautiful things; there were flowers and trees
There were bevies of birds and swarms of bees;
There were cities and temples and towers; and these
  All pictured in silver sheen.

I studied the silver sheen on my window very closely every morning, marvelling at the tiny patterns, and entering into the imaginative world of the poet.

It was not so bad sleeping in a freezing cold bedroom when there was so much magic in the air.

The school was also very cold. There were no radiators and the only heating in the classrooms was an open coal fire. If you were lucky enough to have a desk on that side of the room, you might be able to feel a little of the warmth, but the rest of the room was icy. It was hard to hold your pencil when your hands were blue with cold.

When the school milk was delivered during the morning, the cold crates were put round the fire to warm them. You could tell which bottles were frozen, because the milk had expanded and lifted the bottle tops. The frozen bottles were put closest to the fire.

The weather got colder and colder, and then came the snow. It fell steadily during the night and by morning Radwell was transformed. I'd never really seen snow before – not like this anyway. We'd had snow in London in a previous winter and everybody wanted to build a snowman and throw snowballs, but the thin covering of snow barely covered the dirty pavements, and our snowballs were dirty gritty lumps.

This was different. I ran out into the garden and it was so deep that you couldn't walk properly. Your feet made deep holes in the snow but you didn't get to the bottom of it. It was very exciting. We couldn't even open the garden gate. Uncle 'erbert got the big shovel and started to clear the garden path. There was enough snow to make the biggest snowman you could want – and it was still snowing.

The whole area was hidden under a deep white blanket, and the snow, driven by the strong north-east wind, had been blown against the hedges making it even deeper. These were called snowdrifts. It must have been ten or twelve feet deep at the side of the road and you couldn't see where the ditches were.

The lanes were impassable. Nothing could get into Radwell and no one could get out. We were snowed in and completely cut off from the outside world. It was really quite exciting. There was no bus to Baldock so we couldn't get to the shops, and the mobile grocery van would not be able to make its weekly visit. We would have to be self-sufficient.

People who live in isolated areas are prepared for this kind of situation and Auntie Edie was no exception. The larder was full. It was stocked with tins of soup and vegetables, bags of rice and dried beans. There was suet and flour for making puddings and dried fruit for cakes. It was like a grocer's shop – even better because there were Auntie Edie's homemade jams and bottled fruit.

I don't know how Mum would have managed because she could never afford to buy extra food. We ate everything as fast as she could buy it, and there was barely enough to last us for a week. Dad used to get his 'dole' money on Thursdays, so Wednesdays were always difficult. She didn't have enough money to buy eggs or meat or expensive things until the following day. Sometimes by Wednesday evening we didn't have a penny for the gas meter. When the gas ran out, the light would dim and there was only just enough gas to keep the pilot light going. We would spend the evening with a dim flickering light for the want of a penny, and of course, the gas cooker wouldn't work either. It was very hard for Mum, but she would never borrow. Her first priority was to pay the rent and we were never in debt. I couldn't imagine how we could ever have filled a store cupboard, but in Radwell it was an absolute necessity. This was in the days before houses had freezers, or even refrigerators, but we had everything we needed and I thought it was wonderful.

We were in a world of our own. The doctor couldn't come if you were ill; Uncle 'erbert couldn't go to work and we couldn't go to school.

I don't know if the whole school was closed. Miss Reddall was already there and the Newnham children would be able to get there, but Mrs Peacock wouldn't be able to come in on her motorbike from Royston.

Mr Payne decided to organise lessons for us in the village hall. We had no desks or books, no blackboard and no interest in learning – at least not learning sums or writing compositions. But teachers are always teachers, and they are never happy unless they are making the children learn. I always liked going to school. I enjoyed lessons and got good marks in my books, but there were other, different things to learn besides classroom lessons.

We paid token respect to the formal education system for a couple of hours, and then we were told we could go out in the snow.

The dell was the place to go. It was in the meadow, just opposite the village hall, next to Rose Cottage, and all you needed was a toboggan. Some appeared miraculously as we were released from the village hall. While we were being detained in our makeshift school, Mr Bedington had been busy.

He lived in the house next to the church, which used to be the vicarage. He must have remembered his childhood and a snowy winter, and he knew that all we needed were a few toboggans. He set to work with hammer and nails, some wood and some rope, and made these wonderful sledges.

The far side of the dell was the best slope. It gave us the longest and fastest ride, and it was exciting and exhilarating.

Many years later the same slope looked like a gentle incline into a small hollow at the edge of the meadow, but in 1940 it was a ski-run which could equal the black runs at St. Moritz.

There were trees on the sides of the dell which had to be avoided, and the log of a fallen tree at the bottom. You had to learn to steer your sledge to avoid these obstacles.

We played in the dell for the rest of the morning, and then, freezing cold, wet and hungry, with rosy cheeks and stinging ears, we went home for lunch.

"What's that lovely smell?" I asked as I got in.

"Auntie Edie is baking bread," said Uncle 'erbert. It was the best bread I have ever tasted. It was still warm and the butter melted as soon as you spread it. And there was homemade vegetable soup to warm us up. There was a roaring fire and we got as close to it as we could until we thawed out.

The next few days it was the same, playing in the snow, making snowmen, having snowball fights and tobogganing. The teachers seemed to forget the idea of school and Radwell was a children's winter paradise. I don't know how long our food supplies would have lasted, but that was not our worry.

It was hard for the farmers, who still had to look after their animals and milk the cows, but with no one being able to collect the milk, they were always pleased to sell it to us. If we took a big jug to the farm we could buy a fresh supply of milk straight from the cow. The chickens were not laying eggs at this time of the year, but we had dried egg powder which could be used in cakes, or served scrambled, or in an omelette.

The snow continued, and the dell was still the best place to go. The toboggan runs were getting better. The tracks were compressed by frequent use and resembled ice rather than snow, and with a thin covering of fresh snow on top of the ice, they became dangerously fast. The rides were even more exhilarating and steering became very difficult. Sooner or later someone was going to have an accident, and it was John. He steered too close to the fallen log, and hitting it, stopped abruptly with his leg caught between the sledge and the tree trunk. We thought he had broken his leg and he was obviously in great pain.

Being isolated, no longer seemed to be quite so attractive. We had no telephone, and even if we could have contacted the doctor, he couldn't have got through to us, nor an ambulance to take him to hospital. It was quite worrying, but he was being very brave – he couldn't let Joan think he was a baby. We helped him back to the house, where Auntie Edie examined his wounds, and said that it was not broken. We were greatly relieved, and began to realise the seriousness of being cut off from the outside world.

We'd had a wonderful time and had enjoyed the deep snow, but our disappointment was tinged with relief when eventually the thaw came and the roads were cleared, and the school bus would again be able to take us to school.

* * * * * * * * *

John had his eleventh birthday at the beginning of January so he was in his final year of Junior School. Miss Reddall arranged for the pupils in the top class to sit the scholarship examination. This was very important because it would determine which school the pupils would go to the following year. There was a secondary school in Ashwell, a mile or two past Newnham, and our school bus went there every morning, but there was no Grammar School or Central School nearby. If John passed the scholarship exam, it would probably mean that he would have to leave Radwell, but we wouldn't know for a few months, until they had marked the papers. He sat the exam – and then we forgot about it.

SPRING

The cold east wind stopped blowing and it began to get warmer. Winter was coming to an end and we were looking forward to spring – then summer. It was so different from London.

In the city, it was quite easy to describe the seasons. Winter was cold with dark evenings and there were no leaves on the trees. Summer was hot and the trees were green – and it was light enough after school to play in the yard until bedtime. Spring and autumn were neither hot nor cold and the leaves were either growing or falling. And that was it.

In the country, something was happening all the time. Birds began to build their nests, and they were all different. Some of them would use twigs and moss to make their nests in the trees, but the house martins built their nest under the eaves of the house, like a little mud hut, leaving a small hole to get in and out. They used to spit on the mud to make it stick together. I thought that was really clever, and was very proud that we had a nest at the back of our house. We could watch the adult birds flying in and out, and eventually the young ones when they were old enough to fly. Rooks and crows built their nests in the highest trees where they thought their eggs would be safe, and ducks and swans made their nests on the river banks or on the island.

Cuckoos are very lazy. They don't bother to make a nest. They find another bird's nest with eggs in, and when the mother bird is away, they lay their own eggs in the nest. Sometimes they lay a lot of eggs, all in different nests, so they don't have to bother to feed their young. When the young cuckoo is hatched, it pushes all the other fledglings or eggs out of the nest where they are left to perish on the ground. The poor mother bird doesn't seem to realise what has happened and she has to feed the young cuckoo. The chicks are very big and hungry, and it is hard for the new mother to bring enough food back to the nest to feed it.

It was Miss Reddall who taught us all this. She knew a lot about nature and encouraged us to take an interest in it. On one occasion she took us into her private garden next to the school, and showed us all the things that were growing there. She knew the names of all the flowers and trees, and showed us the buds on some of the plants. She explained how she had to protect the new growth against slugs and snails, and different insects, and then we went back into the classroom and wrote a composition called '*The Schoolhouse Garden in Spring*'.

On another occasion, she took us on a nature walk. If she heard a bird singing she would stop and say, "Listen! Do you hear that bird?" and she would tell us what it was. All the birds had different songs, not like the London sparrows and pigeons, which didn't really sing. We were soon able to distinguish between the different birds – the blackbird, the song thrush or the lark. If you were close enough to see them, you could recognise different birds by their size and colour – the male blackbird with his orange bill and his brown hen not far away; the big black and white magpies which were always very aggressive towards other birds; and the pretty little blue-tits. You could even recognise some of the birds when they were flying – the swallows and swifts would dive through the air as they caught insects as they flew, and the little lark which went higher and higher until you could hardly see it up in the sky.

We collected frogspawn from the pond and took it back to the classroom to put in our aquarium. It was like a mass of jelly balls, with a little black spot in the middle of each ball, and each week we noticed the changes and drew pictures in our nature books. First the little black bits changed shape and looked like commas and then they grew tails and became moving tadpoles. Each week our drawings recorded the changes as the tadpoles grew four little legs, lost their tails and turned into frogs.

Toad spawn was similar to frogspawn except that it was in a long string instead of being in a mass.

One of the birds which we didn't hear when we were out on our nature walks was the yellowhammer.

"You must listen out for it," said Miss Reddall in the classroom, "You won't be able to mistake it – it has a very distinctive song. It sings its song all on one note, except for the last note and it sounds as though it is saying 'A little bit of bread and no cheese'." She then began to sing these words as though she was the bird; dropping her voice about two tones on the last word. I couldn't imagine hearing a bird which sounded as though it were talking. More than twenty-five years later, on our way to a family holiday in Cornwall, we stopped on Salisbury Plain to fly my son's kite. And there it was.

"Listen," I said, "Listen to that bird!" We all stopped and listened.

"It's a yellowhammer, and it's saying 'A little bit of bread and no cheese'!" It was quite unmistakeable. I recognised it at once. Miss Reddall was right. It did sound as though it was talking. I wondered what she would have thought if she had known that I was still benefiting from her teaching after so many years. I know now that I owe more to Miss Reddall than to any other teacher I ever had and I am still grateful to her. She taught me to love the countryside and to respect it. She made me aware of the living things around me, and helped to develop in me empathy for the animals. Radwell was so different from London. Another evacuee whose letter home can be seen in the Imperial War Museum summed it up beautifully by writing "Down here they have a thing called Spring. It happens every year".

* * * * * * * * * *

John's examination results came through, and he had passed. He had won a scholarship to a Central School. If he had gone to the elementary school in Ashwell, he would have left school when he was fourteen, which was the official school-leaving age, but at the Grammar Schools and the Central Schools, you were expected to stay on till you were sixteen to take General School Certificate (GSC). The most able pupils then continued in the sixth form for a further two years to take Higher School Certificate (HSC) which was a requirement for entry to University.

John would have to leave Radwell at the end of the summer term. It was assumed that the war would end before he had finished his schooling so it was important to choose a London school within reasonable travelling distance from home. Barnsbury School was only three or four miles from Holborn, and as it had been evacuated to Hitchin it seemed an ideal choice. A new billet would be found for him and he would leave Radwell in the summer holidays.

WINSTON CHURCHILL

Radwell was calm and peaceful and it was difficult to realise that there was a war on. People were still calling it

'The Phoney War' because we had not been attacked, and many wondered if the evacuation had been necessary. There was a gradual drift of evacuees back to the cities, and some who had gone back home for Christmas had decided not to return. It was estimated that by Christmas, one third of the evacuees had gone home.

From time to time we had reminders that we were still at war. We listened to the news every day on the wireless.

In May, Hitler invaded Belgium and Holland, and Neville Chamberlain resigned. Winston Churchill became the new Prime Minister and although he was already sixty-five years old, we had confidence in him, and believed he would lead us to an early victory. He said,

"I have nothing to offer but blood, toil, tears and sweat. You ask what is our aim? I can answer that in one word: victory ....."

Winston Churchill May 1940

He said the things we wanted to hear and we were filled with hope. He sounded very positive and reassuring. His manner was authoritative and he inspired confidence. He didn't say it would be easy but he made us believe that we were safe in his hands; and that we would win in the end. We now had a dynamic leader that we could trust, and morale was high.

His strong words were soon followed by action. He immediately formed a coalition Government with a War Cabinet drawn from talent in all the major political parties Within a week, groups known as Local Defence Volunteers were being organised (later to become the Home Guard) to mobilise the labour force which had not been conscripted into the Armed Services. They were to play an important role on the Home Front, throughout the war.

More evidence of Churchill's leadership came later in the same month, with the directive to remove all signposts in the country. Street nameplates were taken down, place names were removed from all towns and villages, and signs giving directions to them were also taken down. There was a danger, we were told, that enemy spies would be dropped by parachute, and would want to get their bearings. If anybody was to ask us the way to anywhere, we were instructed not to tell them. It was most likely that they would want to get to London and I decided that if anybody asked me how to get there, I was going to point them up the Great North Road. Nobody ever asked me.

A lot of emphasis was put on the possibility of spies being amongst us. We were always being reminded on the wireless not to give away any secrets as this could endanger the lives of others. Advertisements and poster campaigns urged us to be careful.

'*Walls have ears', 'Careless talk costs lives'* and so on. We were told that we had to be extra careful in Radwell because of the Army regiment being based in the White House. They were fairly well hidden away at the bottom of the lane and you would think nobody could find them, but occasionally army vehicles went in and out of the village and could be seen on the main road. The Regiment based there was the Royal Signals, and more conspicuous than their movements was the high radio receiver mast which they had erected in the meadow at the top of the lane.

Raw recruits were being trained to be radio operators before being sent to the war front. They were an essential military force both in attacking the enemy and in defending our shores. German intelligence would have loved to have disrupted their training, and secrecy about their location was paramount.

France had already been invaded and in June they surrendered, signing an armistice with Germany. Many of the ordinary French people did not agree with this, and were not happy, and an underground resistance movement was formed.

General de Gaulle strongly opposed the French collaboration with Germany and refused to accept the authority of the Vichy government. He escaped to England, and was the self-appointed leader of the 'FREE FRENCH'. He worked closely with Churchill throughout the war although there were times when they disagreed on strategy.

It was encouraging to have the support of this important Frenchman and the resistance movement, but Hitler was very powerful and the Germans in occupied France were too close to us. They were just a short distance across the channel and we felt very threatened.

The first attack on England came in August 1940 in what became known as 'THE BATTLE OF BRITAIN'. German aircraft flew across the channel making massive attacks on British airfields, but were fought off by our spitfires. The RAF pilots in their small manoeuvrable planes fought magnificently to protect our shores and eventually the Germans stopped their attacks. Winston Churchill paid tribute to the bravery of our pilots when he said,

"Never in the field of human conflict was so much owed by so many to so few."

Winston Churchill August 1940

POISONOUS BERRIES

After the Battle of Britain there was a lull and in the peace of the countryside I could forget the war and again marvel at the beauty of nature, and the ever-changing scene. The blossom on the trees had fallen and the fruit was ripening. The corn was turning gold and the farmers began to harvest their crops. Everywhere you looked there were things waiting to be eaten. There was fruit on the trees, nuts in the woods, mushrooms in the fields, and berries in the hedgerows. And it was all free. Hips and haws were very disappointing. They were furry inside and not juicy and you couldn't really eat them. Beechnuts were quite nice, but they were difficult to open and too small to bother about. Cobnuts and hazel nuts were very good. Crab apples were a waste of time. If you wanted an apple, it was better to climb a fence and get a decent one from an orchard. Mushrooms had to be taken home to be cooked, but you couldn't eat toadstools. I liked sloes. They were dark blue and were like very small plums. The stones were far too big for the fruit, so there wasn't much flesh to eat, but you had a very strange sensation when you ate one. They weren't sour, but they made your mouth go very dry. It was a funny feeling but I quite liked it. You couldn't eat many sloes. Blackberries were favourites, although the best ones were always just out of reach, and you couldn't eat many blackberries without getting covered in scratches. There was always something to tempt me. There were lots of berries I didn't know the names of, small brown berries, big red berries and they were all worth a try.

Scouring the woodlands and the hedgerows for free food was quite tiring. When I got back to Auntie Edie's I wanted to lie down.

"Auntie Edie, can I go to bed, please?"

"No," she replied, "Don't go to bed."

I was very surprised, because she usually let me do what I wanted. "I'm very tired," I insisted.

"No," she repeated, "It's too early. If you go to bed now, you won't sleep tonight."

I didn't know how I was going to stay awake. I could hardly stand up. And then, suddenly it happened. I was violently sick. I was going to go outside to the toilet but Auntie said, "No, go upstairs and use the potty in your bedroom."

I went upstairs and sat on the pot while Auntie Edie cleared up the mess. I sat there for ages swaying backwards and forwards and still wanting to lie down. I was very sick. It took Auntie Edie quite a while to clear up downstairs. When she had finished, she called up to me, "Is there any more?"

I looked at the floor in front of me at the remains of my stomach and called back, "Yes, it's on the floor up here."

When Auntie Edie saw me sitting on the pot, she just said "Ohh!" very slowly, and I immediately realised that I was not supposed to be sitting on the pot, but using it to be sick in. Poor Auntie Edie, I realised again that she was not very pleased with me, but she didn't complain or reprimand me in any way.

"You'd better lie down for a little while," was all she said, and she let me stay there until I felt better.

I've never been sure what I had eaten that had upset me, but I learned later than one of the berries was called Deadly Nightshade, and I laid the blame on the big black juicy berries that I had eaten. Obviously I had eaten something poisonous.

* * * * * * * * *

By now all the young birds had flown from their nests and some were getting ready to fly away. I knew that not all of our birds live in England all the year round, and in late summer, before it gets too cold, they fly thousands of miles to warmer countries, like Spain or Africa. But they come back again in spring. No one really knows how they find their way but they come back to the same place. They didn't seem to come to London. All we ever seemed to have were sparrows and pigeons.

The swallows and martins go, and so do the cuckoos. Miss Reddall taught us a song:

> *Cuckoo, Cuckoo*
> *Pray what d'you do?*
> *In April I open my bill*
> *In May I sing night and day*
> *In June I change my tune*
> *In July away I fly*
> *In August, away I must.*

> *Cuckoo, Cuckoo*
> *Pray where d'you go?*
> *Up high into the sky*
> *Far way over the sea*
> *To Spain I fly again*
> *Day and Night, I take my flight*
> *Cuckoo, goodbye to you.*

The summer was drawing to a close and it wasn't only the cuckoo that I had to say goodbye to. John was leaving Radwell to go to Hitchin, about eight miles away, and he was going to be billeted with Mr and Mrs Palmer in Bearton Road. I hoped they would be kind foster parents, and that he would like his new school. I was going to miss him very much but you have to accept separation when there's a war on.

The beautiful voice of Vera Lynn could be heard on the wireless, giving us hope and comfort, and reminding us that our separation was a shared experience which must be faced with courage.

We'll meet again, don't know where, don't know when,
But I know we'll meet again, some sunny day.
Keep smiling through, just like you always do,
'Til the blue skies drive the dark clouds far away.

So will you please say hello to the folks that I know,
Tell them I won't be long.
They'll be happy to know that as you saw me go,
I was singing this song.

We'll meet again, don't know where, don't know when,
But I know we'll meet again, some sunny day.

John left Radwell and I did not know when I would see him again.

Vera Lynn was gaining in popularity and she travelled through India to Burma entertaining the troops. She appeared regularly on the radio throughout the year in her own programme called 'Sincerely Yours'. She was criticised by some of the politicians who believed that the content of her programme was bad for morale as it would make the troops homesick.

I would be all right without John, because I was lucky to have

Auntie Edie and Uncle 'erbert. They put the camp bed away and I slept in the big double bed.

THE BLITZ

The Battle of Britain had given us a warning that the 'Phoney War' was coming to an end. On September 7th 1940, we were in no doubt. The real war had started. The first air raid siren sounded at 8.45pm and for the next two and a half hours, enemy aircraft flew over London dropping their heavy bombs. This was the beginning of 'The Blitz'.

Every evening, under cover of darkness, they came back, night after night for two months, targeting London and other big cities. We listened every morning to the news on the wireless, hearing of the devastation and the damage which was being caused. Coventry Cathedral suffered a direct hit and was almost completely demolished. London was always under attack, the prime targets being railway stations and major junctions, docks, munitions factories and anywhere which would disrupt our war effort.

In the densely populated areas, it was inevitable that many bombs fell on residential properties killing innocent civilians and destroying over 300,000 homes. Night after night, the raids continued and all we could do was listen to the news each morning on the wireless.

I worried about Mum and Dad, and hoped they were all right. We had no telephone, and neither had they. There was no way of finding out. Even if they had survived the previous night's raid, and were still alive, for how long would they be able to survive? They might not be lucky every night, and I feared for their safety. It was very frightening. I didn't know what I would do if anything happened to them.

I thought about Joan Bovingdon, who hadn't got a Mum, and realised that I could end up without a Mum or Dad. If I went back to London, after the war, and they weren't there, I wouldn't know where to go. I couldn't expect to stay here. Auntie Edie and Uncle 'erbert were very nice but they didn't have to look after me once the war ended.

I didn't realise at the time that the government had foreseen this problem, and accepted that some of the evacuees would be orphaned. A memo was circulated in 1939, asking:

> **How can the child be put in touch with the next of kin or some friend if both parents should, for example, be killed?**
>
> **Memo Ev5**
> **Minister of Health 1939**

I thought of what we had been told at the beginning of the war ... "It is of vital importance to preserve the lives of children who will be the citizens of the next generation" Well – they might have thought that was a good idea but they hadn't asked the children – and if they had asked me, I had different ideas. I thought the most important thing was for families to be together. I wanted the whole of my family to survive, but if some were going to be killed, it would be better if we all died together. I wanted to live but not if Mum and Dad weren't there. The baby was lucky because he was always living with Mum. I felt very strongly about this and I'm quite sure that many other evacuees must have felt the same.

Auntie and Uncle, and Miss Reddall must have known we were worried but nobody said anything. We just listened to the wireless every morning and hoped everything would be all right. I never told anybody about my fears, and that I thought they should have kept families together. Nobody ever asks the children.

Not surprisingly, the relentless bombardment of London and the big cities led to a second wave of evacuation. This was no time for complacency, and the city was not the place to be. People flocked back to the safe area in their thousands – anywhere – to get away from the bombing. There was less time to organise transport and reception centres than in the previous year, and the billeting officers had to work on an ad hoc basis. Some people returned to the areas where they had been evacuated originally, and others left the cities for the first time.

One such family arrived in Radwell. A crowd of people carrying suitcases and bags came down the lane in the middle of the afternoon. I couldn't imagine how they had got here, because there was no bus at that time of day. They looked tired and weary, especially one of the ladies who was limping. There were six or seven of them. I was very curious to know where they would be going because they had a little girl with them. She was very pretty, with fair curly hair, and looked about my own age.

The man seemed to be in charge, and he stopped outside our Council Cottages, at Number 4. Well, they couldn't stay with Mrs Lilley, because she already had a houseful. There was Mr and Mrs Lilley and Ken, and Alma, as well as the evacuees, Beryl Marchant and Beryl's mother. All her bedrooms were full.

The man knocked at the door and spoke to Mrs Lilley, and then he beckoned to the ladies and the little girl, and they all went in.

Everybody was curious to know who they were, and why they had come to Radwell. I decided to go out to the pump to get a bucket of water. The pump was shared by the six cottages, and was nearest to the back of Mrs Lilley's house. If anybody came out of her back door to go to the toilet, I would be able to see them. The back door was open and the little girl was the first to come out.

I smiled at her as I started to fill my bucket and she came towards me.

"What's your name?" I asked, shyly.

"Brenda Bennett," she replied. "What's yours?"

"I'm June Matthews. I'm an evacuee, and I live in Number 2 with Mr and Mrs Edwards, but I call them Uncle 'erbert and Auntie Edie. They're very nice."

Brenda was quite pretty, and had a very friendly face, and I hoped she would be staying. It would be good to have a friend living so close.

"How old are you?" I asked.

"Nine," she replied, "How old are you?"

"I'm eight and a quarter." I said, trying to make it sound as though I was nearly nine. I looked at her fair curly hair. It was very tightly curled, quite frizzy, and it reminded me a bit of Rosalyn's hair, and I wondered if her comb got stuck when she tried to comb it.

"I saw your Dad knock at Mrs Lilley's door," I said, "Does he know her?"

"That's not my Dad – that's my Uncle, my Dad's still in London. He couldn't come because he's got to work. My Mum's here, and my two aunts, and their mum."

"Why have you come here?"

"We'd been sleeping in the air-raid shelter because of all the bombing, and this morning when we came out, everything around us was on fire. The whole of the sky was bright red. I live on the Isle of Dogs, and we were all scared. My Dad said, 'They'll keep bombing here until they've destroyed the docks. I've got to get you all out of here.' My uncle said he knew someone who lived in the country, so my Dad told us to pack our bags as quickly as we could. He got a lorry and drove us to Kings Cross Station, and we got a train to Baldock."

"How did you get here from Baldock – there's no bus at this time of the afternoon?"

"We had to walk, and it was very hard for my Mum because of her arthritis."

"And are you all going to stay with Mrs Lilley?"

"I don't think so, but we're staying there tonight, until they can find us somewhere. She's going to make us up some beds on the floor."

"I hope you do stay here – it's nice here. This is our pump, where we get our water. It's much better than across the lane where they've got a well. You have to throw the first bucketful away in the morning because it always comes out brown. It's the rust in the pipes. After that, it comes out a bit white, but that's only chalk and it doesn't hurt you. Do you want to have a go? You have to pump the handle up and down. It's quite easy." Brenda got hold of the handle and filled the bucket. I knew that if she stayed in Radwell, she would be my friend.

The next morning there was a lot of activity in the village. Brenda told me that they had made her a bed on two chairs and that the others had slept on the floor. It was quite crowded and they hadn't been very comfortable, but at least they felt safe. They were all very grateful to Mrs Lilley but they were hoping that they would find somewhere with a bit more space before nightfall.

The Royal Signals came to the rescue. Someone had the idea of going to the White House to ask the Army if they could help, and they responded to the challenge with enthusiasm. They erected an enormous marquee on the green next to the village hall, with camp beds, blankets and an army survival kit, and Brenda and her family had a place to live until somewhere more permanent could be found.

Eventually, billets were found for Brenda's uncle, aunts, and their mother in Hinksworth, a neighbouring village, and Mrs Lilley agreed to take Brenda and her mother. Mr and Mrs Lilley moved out of their big bedroom and gave it to the four evacuees, so Brenda and her mother were sharing with the Marchants.

I was delighted when I realised that Brenda would be living at Number 4. There were no other girls of my age in the village, the local girls and the evacuees were all older than me. Brenda was living so close and she was going to be my friend.

"I'll show you where we catch the school bus, we have to be on the corner of the Stotfold lane by eight o'clock. Our teacher is Miss Reddall. I'll ask her if you can sit next to me."

Brenda was nine months older than me, and as her birthday was in August, she was not in my school year, but all the juniors were in the same classroom, so we could sit and work together.

"Wait till you see the lavs," I said to her, "There are no chains to pull and there are not even any buckets. Everything just slides down the slope and goes into the field behind. It's freezing cold in the winter, especially when it's windy."

Of course, Brenda would soon have discovered the delights of the school toilets for herself, and all the other places of local interest that I showed her, but I was determined that she was going to be my friend. I was not going to give anyone else a chance to monopolise her and she seemed quite happy to be with me. We got on well, right from the start – we worked together and played together and became almost inseparable. She was the first real friend I ever had.

The author, with Pat Middlemass (left) and Brenda Bennett

"You can join the choir," I told her, and Mr Turner, the organist and choirmaster was pleased to have another soprano to swell the ranks. "And you'll be able to pump the organ as well."

A wooden handle had to be pumped up and down to fill the organ chamber with air. A brass weight on a string indicated the volume of air in the chamber. When it was full, the weight would drop to the bottom, and you could stop pumping for a while and watch the weight slowly rise as the organ was being played. It was important to pump more air in before the weight reached the red warning line on the frame.

I remember with some embarrassment, the time when my concentration lapsed and my thoughts had wandered. I was suddenly brought back to my responsibility by the sound of the organ as it began to play out of tune. I could see Brenda and the others desperately trying to stifle their laughter as they hid their faces behind their hymnbooks.

We went to Sunday School together, which was held in the Mill House. This eighteenth century manor house was an imposing timber clad building overlooking the lake. It was set in 4 acres of land, and to get to it we had to go through the lane in the woods, past the notice board which said '*PRIVATE ROAD – NO THOROUGHFARE – Trespassers will be prosecuted*'.

The house had three entrances. The lessons were given by Mrs de Zoote, and we became familiar with all the Bible stories.

On one occasion, Brenda excelled herself and covered herself in glory.

"Who can tell me," asked Mrs de Zoote, at the beginning of the lesson, "what was the name of the High Priest I told you about at the end of last week's lesson?"

Brenda put up her hand, "Caiaphas," she said.

"Well done, Brenda," said Mrs de Zoote, obviously impressed, and Brenda smiled with satisfaction. I thought she was very clever.

We spent most of our time together, either working or playing. We explored the countryside, and knew all the byways and footpaths for miles around. When we couldn't think of where to go, or what to do, we would sit in the meadow and make daisy-chains. Brenda's father came to visit her, and planned to take her to the cinema in Baldock. This was a rare treat, but still Brenda wanted to be with me.

"Can June come with us?" she asked her father, and he agreed.

It was wonderful to have such a good friend and the trials and tribulations of war were almost forgotten.

* * * * * * * * * *

My other friend was Trixie, the dog. I loved the way she used to greet me when I came home from school. She jumped up, wagging her tail, wanting to lick me. I felt very special. We played ball together, or I would throw a stick for her in the garden. She never brought back the wrong stick. Her eyes were big and brown and you could tell by the way she looked up at Uncle 'erbert that she loved him best.

Trixie was a very gentle dog, a bit over-weight and friendly with everyone. She spent most of her time curled up in her basket. One evening she would not settle. She whined and cried, and was clearly agitated. She wanted to go into the scullery, and went straight to the kitchen sink.

"There must be a mouse in there, come in from the garden," said Auntie Edie.

"I'll catch it," I volunteered. I wasn't frightened of mice. I was going to catch it and put it out in the garden. There was a small space behind the cupboard, and according to Trixie, that's where the mouse was.

"Push that end of the cupboard close to the wall, so it can't get out that way," I said, "And when I'm ready, pull it out a bit on this side." The mouse would then be trapped in a small area. All I had to do was to block the exit, and cup it in my hands.

I crawled under the sink and they pulled out the cupboard as I had suggested. I had the exit covered and was ready. Well, I was not ready for what I saw. It was a huge rat, standing on two legs and stretching up. And it was looking at me. We were eyeball to eyeball.

"It's a rat!" I screamed. I knew that rats were dangerous and would attack if they were cornered. 'They can dive at your face or your throat' I had been told. My face was too close, and I crawled out from under the sink as fast as I could. I did not want it to get me, so for safety, I ran terrified into the bathroom, which was next to the scullery, and locked myself in.

I could hear lots of activity in the scullery, until finally Auntie and Uncle said,

"It's all right, you can come out now. Trixie got it."

I emerged sheepishly from the bathroom, to see the floor, the cupboard, the walls, everywhere splattered with blood. Trixie had caught it and shaken it like a rag doll until it was dead.She had earned everyone's respect and admiration, and of course, some extra chocolate buttons. They talked about her heroic act for weeks afterwards, saying that they did not think she was capable of such aggression.

"Who's a clever girl then, Trixie?" they would ask, and although they frequently talked about it between themselves, and to friends and neighbours, not once was my hasty exit referred to. I am in no doubt, they kept that as a private joke out of my hearing.

CLOTHES RATIONING

The war dragged on, and all hopes of an early peace faded. Sometimes it seemed as though it would never end. We were dependent upon the wireless for news of what was happening but did not always get the full picture. When our armies were

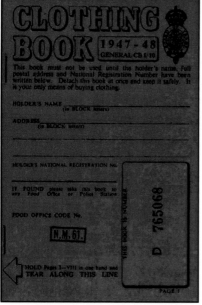

advancing, the news was detailed and jubilant. We thought we were winning and morale was high. At other times the news was less optimistic, but we were never given the full details of our losses or retreats. We were protected from bad news and we were left to guess. The absence of good news implied bad news.

One aspect of the war which could not be kept from us was the shortage of raw materials. In June 1941, clothes rationing was introduced. We were allowed sixty-six coupons per year, but with eleven coupons needed for a dress and five for a pair of shoes, the coupons did not go far. Fashions were determined by the shortages and nothing was wasted. Skirts were made without pleats and were not gathered or flared, and trousers were made without turn-ups.

A big campaign was launched to 'Make Do And Mend', and women were encouraged to unravel worn-out jumpers and re-knit them, and to make children's clothes from worn-out adult garments.

It was not only clothes that were in short supply. It was everything. There was a shortage of soap, and coupons were issued for petrol. The depleted workforce resulted in a shortage of home-produced coal, and imports were equally scarce owing to a heavy loss of shipping. We were told to save gas and electricity and one of the ways of achieving this was to use less hot water. We were allowed only five inches of bath water. Nobody could check this, of course, but we all wanted to make our 'war effort'. Some people painted a line round the bath at the five-inch level to remind them of the limit. I never really understood how having a shallow bath,

or switching off the lights could make any difference. Nobody ever explained to me the link between hot water or electricity, and the shortage of coal, but like everyone else I wanted to help and I accepted it.

Nothing was wasted. We were not to put more food on our plates than we could eat and we should eat what we had been given.

Everything that could be used again was recycled. Waste paper was collected, as were tins and silver paper. Bones were used to make glue, and aluminium was a valuable source of material for making aeroplanes. Anything edible was collected in pig bins.

Everybody, from the oldest to the youngest, was encouraged to save. A friend who was in the infants' school at the time, recalls how his teacher made them save paper. Margins were not allowed, as writing had to go the edge of the page. Only one sheet of paper was given out at a time, and when it was filled on both sides, it had to be shown to the teacher before another sheet was issued. If the teacher spotted any wasted space, she would write 'H.H.' in the offending area.

"And what does 'H.H.' stand for?" she would ask, and they all knew it stood for 'Helping Hitler'!

The shortage that affected us most directly was food. Supplies were closely monitored, and when stocks were low, the value of food coupons was adjusted accordingly, and women often found it difficult to provide an interesting and varied diet.

It was important to maintain high morale amongst ordinary people, especially when shortages were acute, so the government introduced propaganda to encourage and praise housewives as they struggled to feed their families. The Ministry of Food published leaflets giving cookery hints and suggesting ways of making nourishing meals with minimum ingredients, and housewives were praised for their efforts.

THE BRITISH HOUSEWIFE is helping to make a second front – the Kitchen Front – against Hitler. That is why we say "Medals for you, Madam." *Is there anything else you can do?* Read the list of awards below and see how many your household deserves. *More* medals for you, Madam!

A Medal for this . . .
Making delicious dishes from home-grown vegetables, with just a *flavouring* of meat or fish.

A Medal for this . . .
Trying new things – fresh salted cod for instance – acting on recipes and hints from Kitchen Front Wireless Talks, Food Advice Centres and Ministry of Food Magazine Announcements.

A Medal for this . . .
Saving all bread crusts and crumbs, taking the crumbs off plates, drying them in the oven and making crisp rusks or crumbs to use in cooking.

A Medal for this . . .
Never accepting more than the rations; and going without rather than pay unfairly high prices for foods that may be scarce.

A Medal for this . . .
Serving larger portions of vegetables than usual; because more are needed to get the same amount of nourishment that used to be had from the scarcer, concentrated kind of foods. Serving three or four different kinds of vegetables at the same meals, and dressing them up with different sauces to get variety.

Ministry of Food, 1941

99

It was considered to be very important to win the co-operation of housewives who were bearing the brunt of the severe rationing, and campaigns like this gave them simultaneously a challenge and a reward. Everybody's contribution to the war on the Home Front was recognised, and the resulting sense of camaraderie always helped to raise morale.

* * * * * * * * * *

In the autumn of 1941 the war entered its third year. In June, Hitler had turned his attention to Russia, but it was not until October that the plight of millions of Russians began to filter through to us. They were starving, and dying on an enormous scale. They were far worse off than we were, and desperately in need of help.

Mr Churchill's wife, Clementine, was the Chairman of the Red Cross, and she launched the 'Aid to Russia Fund'. The target, we were told, was one million pounds in one year, to provide them with essential food, clothing and medical supplies. Everybody responded. People organised fundraising activities. Moiseiwitsch, a Russian pianist living in the West, gave piano recitals, and an England versus Wales football match was organised. On a smaller scale, there were auctions, bring-and-buy sales and collections. Schoolchildren were asked to save their pennies, and weekly collections were made. The target of one million pounds was reached in three months, but the appeal for funds continued. In spite of our efforts to help, Russia eventually suffered the heaviest casualties of the war.

* * * * * * * * * *

Our third war-time Christmas was approaching. In December 1941, the USA joined in the war as our allies, and this gave us renewed hope for an early end to hostilities. World shortages were more acute than ever, and a 'points' system of food rationing was introduced. Ration books continued for specified items, but other foods in short supply were given a points rating, and you could spend the points how you liked. A new product arrived on the market called SPAM. It was a meat substitute and its name was an abbreviation of 'spiced ham'. It did not seem to contain much meat, but could be eaten cold in salads or sandwiches, and could form the basis of a hot meal when served as fritters. This was one of the products available with points.

The months passed and the war dragged on. Our hopes of a quick victory with the help of the USA seemed to have been in vain. We listened to the wireless, and heard of successful bombing raids in Germany, and troops advancing. Then, when things were not going our way, the messages were not so clear, and again we were left to guess. We were told only what they wanted us to know. They could not easily conceal our losses at home, and we were aware of the bombing and devastation in our cities.

Dad was still in London and I worried about him, but Mum was now evacuated with Basil to Letchworth. This was only a few miles away and I was able to visit her occasionally. There was a bus from Baldock to Letchworth, which passed through Norton, and I could get there by walking across the fields.

Mum was billeted with Mrs Cruise, and did the housework in return for her keep. She was not there for long, but it was good to be able to see her and Basil, who was now nearly five and growing fast.

I remember one visit very clearly – or to be more precise, I remember the journey home. As I said goodbye to Mum at the bus-stop, she gave me half-a-crown for pocket money. I kissed them goodbye and got on the bus. When I reached Norton, I crossed to the footpath to start my walk across the fields. I suddenly realised that I had lost my half-a-crown. I was quite sure that I had it when I got off the bus, and that I had not left it on the seat, so I must have dropped it. I retraced my steps to the bus-stop, keeping my eyes always on the path. I had walked through some long grass and felt quite sure it must be there. I walked backwards and forwards brushing the grass aside with my foot, I could not afford to lose half-a-crown. I do not know how long I searched, but with my eyes always looking down, I did not notice how dark it was getting. When I looked up, the trees looked black against an indigo sky, and I was frightened. I abandoned my search and set off on the first part of my journey.

I followed the footpath across a field to a road, where I had to pass a row of houses before crossing the stile to the next field. I had to cross this field to go through the woods. By now, everything looked black and I thought there might be a bogey-man in the woods. I wished I had stayed on the bus till Baldock. It was a longer walk, but it would have been along the main road and not through the woods. I started to cry, but knew I had to keep going. I kept walking and crying very loudly, past the cottages until suddenly a door opened, and a woman asked what was the matter.

"I've got to walk to Radwell. It's dark and I'm frightened that there might be a bogey-man in the woods."

She turned and called to her husband. "Jack, would you take this little girl across the fields to Radwell? She's frightened of the dark."

Jack put on his boots and coat and came with me. Our route took us across the field, through the woods, across the old iron bridge, then through the cornfields behind the White House to Radwellbury Farm. Back in the lane, I looked with relief at the Council Cottages, glad to be home. But I did not want Auntie Edie and Uncle 'erbert to know that I had been frightened and crying, or that I had been brought home by a kind stranger.

"We're nearly there now," I said to Jack. "I live in those Council Cottages. I'll be all right now, thanks. You can go now."

And Jack smiled and said goodbye, and turned to walk home. I would like to have gone back next day to thank the kind couple for their help, but I was too ashamed of myself. I did not tell anyone what had happened, not even Brenda.

THE FACTS OF LIFE

Sometimes the boys could be very, very rude. They did things which were really quite disgusting – things which I did not think girls would do, although they made them laugh. Two of the boys found an unusual way of making some extra pocket money.

"We've got something to show you," they said, "but you'll have to pay one penny. It's going to be down in the woods."

"What is it?" I asked.

"We're not telling you. If you want to know, you'll have to come down to the woods, and pay us your penny first."

A crowd of us went down the lane. When we got to the lake, they told us to wait on the bridge until they were ready. I was not sure if I was going to give them a penny, but I had taken one with me, just in case.

One of them went behind a tree, dropped his trousers and squatted down to do his poo, while the other one kept guard, to keep us away. "Right – we're ready now," they said, "Give us your penny, and you can see it."

I did not think it would be worth a penny, so I waited. Some of the others paid, and were allowed past. The shrieks of surprise, and the laughter persuaded me that it must be worth the money, so I paid up.

I was directed to go behind the tree, and there on a small piece of ground, cleared of leaves, was a steaming pile of poo.

"You have to look closely," they said. I approached the heap with caution, not wanting to smell it, nor to be pushed into it. Then I saw it. The whole heap was moving. It was a writhing mass, full of tiny white worms, all stuck in the poo and struggling to get out. There must have been hundreds of them. Those near the surface had got their heads free, and they wriggled furiously as they tried to release the rest of their tiny bodies. It gave the impression that the whole heap was on the move. I shrieked with surprise and disgust like the others, and giggled as I joined them. I don't know what Miss Reddall would have thought. She was always teaching us about nature, and we had watched the frogs' spawn growing into wriggling tadpoles before they grew little legs and turned into frogs. I did not know if these little tiny worms would grow legs and turn into something, but we would never know because when the show was over, the boys scraped the surrounding ground with their feet, covering the heap with leaves and soil, leaving the little worms no chance of escape. Miss Reddall, and the other grown-ups knew nothing about this spectacle, but it was a real lesson never to be forgotten, and quite good value for a penny.

* * * * * * * * * *

It was at about this time that a greater interest in the rude parts of the body was being explored. Some of the older children would be laughing and sniggering together, excluding me from their conversation. Of course, I wanted to know what they were talking about, so that I could join in.

"You're too young," they teased, "You wouldn't understand." But even though they thought I was too young, they were eager to tell me. I think they wanted to shock me, and to see how I would react.

"We know how babies are born," they boasted. Well, I already knew that. I knew about birds laying eggs, and cows having calves, and if you were a girl, you would have babies when you were married.

"I know," I replied, "they come from inside you. They grow inside the mother, and when they are ready, they come out."

"Yes, but what makes them grow? What starts it?"

I had to think about that one. I had not really thought about that before. "It's when you're grown up, when you're married," I decided.

"We knew you didn't really know. It's what the man does!"

"What does he do?"

"The seed comes out of the man's willie and he puts it inside the woman. He puts his whole willie inside to get the seed out, and that makes it start growing."

I thought about this for a moment. It was another rude episode, like the boys' poo with worms in it, only this time I did not laugh. My Dad would not have done that to my Mum – three times! – and it was an insult to them. Suddenly I seized upon the perfect reply. I thought of Princess Elizabeth and Princess Margaret Rose and said "You don't really think the King and Queen would do that, do you?"

And that was the end of the conversation. Perhaps the older children had just found out, and there was still an element of doubt in their minds. I don't know - but they made no further effort to try to persuade me. I felt that I had won the argument, and almost proved that they were wrong. Yet, in spite of this, they had set me thinking. I thought about it a lot, and I wondered. Could that really be possible? The idea would not go away. I did not believe it, yet I could not entirely dismiss it. There might be an element of truth in it, but I hoped not. It was too embarrassing to think about, and quite disgusting.

* * * * * * * * *

It was now two years since Brenda had arrived in Radwell and she had just had her eleventh birthday. She was born in August, so she was in the class above me, and in September she would be starting at the secondary school in Ashwell. She would have to stay on the bus and I would miss her in lessons, but we could still play together after school, and at the weekends.

Now we were enjoying the long summer holiday, and we could always find something to do. I was surprised, one morning. when she did not appear. We usually met in the lane after breakfast.

"Is Brenda coming out now?" I asked her mother.

"She went out about ten minutes ago," came the reply. I could not imagine where she had gone, nor why she had not called for me. There were not many places where she could be. I wandered down the lane.

"Have you seen Brenda?" I asked Joan.

"Yes, she was going down towards the Church, a few minutes ago."

She was not in the Church. I walked round the churchyard to the back of the church and there she was. She was standing in the corner, crying.

"What's the matter? Why are you crying?"

She was too upset to tell me. "Have you hurt yourself?" She shook her head. "Have you got into trouble?" She shook her head again. I could not imagine what else it could have been. "Then why are you crying?"

"I've got to go," she said.

"Go where?"

"I've got to go back to London. My Dad's got us somewhere else to live, and we're going back."

This was enough to make me cry, too. "Can't you ask if you can stay? Your Mum can go home, and you could stay here."

"No, my Dad wants us all to be together, and we're going on Saturday." Radwell would not be the same without her. Brenda, like me, had come from an inner-city area, with bricks and concrete, noise and soot, and had fallen in love with this peaceful farming area. Some evacuees, like us who had never seen a cow before, found it difficult to adapt to a totally different kind of life, and hankered to get back to the city smoke. But for us, Radwell showed us a beautiful new way of living, where we could watch the ever-changing scene and wonder at the miracles of nature.

* * * * * * * * * *

     I missed Brenda very much, and although I spent more time with the older girls, I often found myself on my own. I sat in the meadow making daisy chains and listened to the birds singing. I tried to remember what Miss Reddall had taught us on our nature walk, to identify the different birds. My thoughts turned to the picture on the classroom wall, with St Francis of Assisi surrounded by the wild animals and the birds. He was my favourite Saint and I wanted to be like him. I wanted the wild animals to trust me like they trusted him.

     I crossed over to the far side of the meadow where there was a big tree near the hedge. Behind the tree were a number of rabbit holes and I had often seen rabbits in that area. I sat down, next to the tree and listened to the birds singing. I leaned against the tree, and made myself comfortable so that I wouldn't fidget. And then I waited. I tried to think calm and peaceful thoughts. I sat very still and talked to the birds and wild animals, not out loud, of course, but in my thoughts. I thought they would know what I was thinking, that they would hear my thoughts. I wanted some rabbits to appear and sit by me, and if a bird were to fly down and sit on my motionless foot, I would not move, but sit very, very still. I sat there, quietly, and I waited. I waited patiently for a long time, breathing quietly and not moving.

     Well – I don't know how St Francis did it, but it didn't work. The rabbits stayed in their burrows and the birds flew away. I've always had the feeling that birds and animals know more than we do – a sixth sense which tells them how to build nests and care for their young; when to fly to a warmer climate and how to get there; Well perhaps they knew that St Francis was a Saint and they knew that I definitely was not!

I wondered if St Francis was with us fifty years later when I stood alongside the late Alan Clark, MP, at Dover docks next to the famous White Cliffs, as we made a silent protest against the export of live animals. We watched as the helpless frightened calves, only a few days old, were driven past us, packed tightly in large lorries on their way to the continent to satisfy the demand for veal. They were followed by old sheep, on their long hot journeys to the abattoirs of southern Europe – Spain, Italy and Greece. The appalling smell, as they stood in their own excrement without food or water, and the pathetic cries of these terrified creatures brought me to tears. Alan Clark put his arm round me but said nothing. I wonder if St Francis was with us, saying a prayer for them, that their suffering would soon be over, and asking forgiveness for those responsible.

We were only a short distance from the White Cliffs of Dover – but where were the bluebirds?

* * * * * * * * * *

It is impossible for me to hear mention of the White Cliffs of Dover without thinking of the bluebirds. They were linked for me inextricably in 1942 when Vera Lynn sang her now famous song.

Vera worked tirelessly throughout the war, travelling round the country and abroad, giving concerts to troops. Earlier, she had been voted 'The Forces Sweetheart' and her songs were being sung by everyone, everywhere.

This is a song of inspiration, and hope for the future with a promise of peace.

> *There'll be Bluebirds over,*
> *The White Cliffs of Dover,*
> *Tomorrow, just you wait and see*
> *There'll be love and laughter,*
> *And peace ever after*
> *Tomorrow, when the world is free.*
>
> *The shepherd will tend his sheep,*
> *The valley will bloom again*
> *And Jimmy will go to sleep,*
> *In his own little room again.*
>
> *There'll be Bluebirds over,*
> *The White Cliffs of Dover,*
> *Tomorrow, just you wait and see!*

'Jimmy' represented all the servicemen who were away from home, away from their mothers, wives and children. Many had already been separated from their families for over three years and there was no indication that the war was coming to an end. This plaintive melody gave them encouragement and hope for the future.

It was not recognised at that time, nor perhaps since, that the evacuees needed this comfort as well. We were the forgotten casualties. Some were exploited or abused; many lost out on their education; all were losers one way or another. Even the lucky ones like me who were happy in their billets and well looked after, had a price to pay.

We lost our carefree childhood with our families. The bond between us and our parents which would have strengthened during six long years, became very fragile. The seven-year-old child who climbed on the coach in 1939 was hardly the same person as the thirteen-year-old adolescent who returned in 1945. Bridges had to be built and adjustments made, and I do not think our plight was ever really recognised.

We were, I believe, the only group of people who were not represented in the Victory Parade in 1946. Everyone was there – the Armed Services, the Red Cross, the Women's Land Army – everyone who had made a contribution during the war except the evacuees.

There were times when we were lonely and homesick, wanting to be at home with our families.

And Vera sang her song. It was my song and it brought tears to my eyes. I listened to it on the wireless until I knew it off by heart, and then sang it over and over again. I changed the words in the middle verse and sang:

And Junie will go to sleep,
In her own little room again.

Now it really was my song. It lightened my darkest hours and gave me hope for a brighter future. It promised us good times ahead when we could grow carnations instead of carrots, and petunias in the place of potatoes; when food would no longer be rationed and there would be bananas in the shops; and when the lights would go on again, bringing the cities back to life after sunset.

It was my favourite song and Vera Lynn was my favourite singer. I tried to sing it like her, and when I heard her on the wireless, I would sing along with her.

It gave me hope, and from then on I was 'Waiting for the Bluebirds'.

AID TO RUSSIA

It's no good feeling sorry for yourself, there are always other people worse off than you are. And we were always being reminded of the plight of the Russians. In spite of the help they had been receiving, they were still in desperate need of warm clothing, food and medical supplies. Thousands had already died – or was it millions? And with the severity of the Russian winter which was just beginning, many more were at risk.

The appeal for Mrs Churchill's 'Aid to Russia Fund' was intensified and we had to help. I did not know whose idea it was, but we, the evacuees, were going to give a concert, and everybody who came would have to pay to see it.

"What sort of concert?" I asked. Joan seemed to know all about it. She was fourteen years old now, and quite grown up.

"Well," she explained, "everyone can be in it. There will be solo items, as well as singing and dancing in groups. Everyone can do what they can. We're going to have a meeting."

It sounded to me as though it was going to be a Variety Show, like the one I had seen with Dad at the Bedford Theatre in Camden Town.

"I'll be the acrobat," I volunteered. I had seen them on stage and thought they were by far the best item in the programme. This was something I could do. My offer was immediately accepted. They had all seen me at school or in the meadow, always doing handstands or cartwheels, or standing on my head. All I had to do was link them together to make a continuous programme.

I measured the width of the stage in pigeon steps and then
marked out a similar distance in the meadow where I planned and
practised a routine. I could start with a handstand, and go right
over to a back-bend, and then do a crab walk followed by a pull-
up. Then I could do another handstand, but this time, end it with
a forward roll. I could hold a headstand for quite a while, bending
one leg to put my foot on my knee, remembering all the time to
stretch and point my toes.

Cartwheels had to be included, I could always do those
in a perfectly straight line, and then a back-drop into a handstand.
I could do a forward handspring, keeping my legs together and
toes pointed, and landing neatly with my feet together. I would
finish up by doing the splits. I would put my head on my forward
knee and stretch my arms to touch my toes, then, still doing the
splits, I would sit up with my arms outstretched and turn to face
the audience – and they would know that was the end. I practised
it, in the meadow over and over again until I was sure I had got it
right.

We called ourselves 'The Petrels' and someone made
some big posters to stick on the walls. We had a few rehearsals to
learn the songs and we were ready for the Big Night.

I did not think many people would come but I peeped
round the curtain before we started and was amazed to see that
the Village Hall was packed. Someone had liaised with the Royal
Signals in the White House, and nearly all the soldiers were there.
One of the soldiers played the piano for us, and the curtain went
up. I watched from the wings, enjoying all the entertainment.

Joan played her Mozart piano piece, 'An Eighteenth
Century Drawing Room', and read a poem called 'A Recipe for a

Bald Head', which she remembers to this day. Doris Van der Wheel sang 'Because' accompanied by the soldier; and Pat Middlemas did some tap dancing. She must have learnt that when she went to her private school. Doris and Jean Hanwell sang 'There's a Hole in my Bucket, Dear Liza', and I did my acrobatic display. It all went without a hitch.

These individual events were interspersed with songs from the chorus. We sang lots of army songs which were greatly appreciated.

> *This is the army, Mister Jones.*
> *No private rooms or telephones.*
> *You had your breakfast in bed before*
> *But you won't have it there any more.*
>
> *This is the army, Mister Green.*
> *We like the barracks nice and clean.*
> *You had a housemaid to clean your floor*
> *But she won't help you out anymore.*
>
> *Do what the buglers command.*
> *They're in the army and not in a band.*
>
> *This is the army, Mister Brown.*
> *You and your baby went to town.*
> *She had you worried, but this is war*
> *And she won't worry you anymore.*

We sang 'The Quarter Master's Stores' and we each sang a solo verse. My verse was:

There are rats, rats, as big as pussy cats
In the stores, in the stores
There were rats, rats, as big as pussy cats
In the Quarter Master's stores

I thought that was a very appropriate verse for me to sing, when I remembered the rat in our scullery.

We had a general sing-song, with the audience joining in all the old favourites, 'Run Rabbit Run', 'Kiss Me Goodnight, Sergeant Major', and of course, 'the Vera Lynn Favourites'.

We ended the show with all of us in the chorus line singing:

Happy days are here again
The skies above are clear again
So let's sing a song of cheer again
Happy days are here again

Altogether shout it now!
There's no one who can doubt it now
So let's tell the world about it now
Happy days are here again

Your cares and troubles are gone;
There'll be no more from now on

Happy days are here again
The skies above are clear again
So let's sing a song of cheer again

Happy days are here again

There was lots of applause, and we had to sing our last song again. Everyone enjoyed the evening, audience and cast alike. As a fund-raising exercise, we must have exceeded our expectations. Mrs Churchill's appeal raised over four million pounds, and we were pleased to have contributed to this figure, but we had no real idea of the size of the problem. Russia suffered more losses during the war than any other country, and it is recorded that they lost more than eleven million military personnel and seven million civilians. I find these statistics quite incomprehensible, even in a World War.

* * * * * * * * * *

1942 was drawing to a close and I would be spending my fourth Christmas away from home.

I was now in the top class of the junior school, and Miss Reddall chose me to be the Virgin Mary in the Nativity Play. It was a great honour. I had to come to Bethlehem with Joseph, and knock on the door of the Inn, where they turned me away. I had to sit in the stable with the animals. The most important part of my performance was to sing a lullaby to the baby doll in my arms.

I had quite a good soprano voice, and was looking forward to my solo:

> *Lu lay thou little tiny child*
> *Bye bye lu lee lu lay*
> *Lu lay thou little tiny child*
> *Bye bye, lu lee lu lay.*

I started singing confidently, knowing that I could sing in tune. Suddenly, in the middle of a line, I swallowed. I don't know where it came from, and I was surprised. I do not remember needing to swallow. It just came on its own. Really, it spoiled my singing. I carried on, as though nothing had happened, but I was disappointed that I had swallowed without wanting to. I knew then, that I could never be a singer and that I would not agree to sing a solo again.

I was all right in the Church choir, it had not happened there, and I enjoyed singing. Auntie Edie and Uncle 'erbert said I was like a bird, always singing around the house, and on Christmas Day in the evening, they wanted me to sing some carols.

"I can sing 'Away in a Manger'," I suggested.

"Stand on the chair," said Uncle 'erbert.

I stood on the wooden chair, and started singing. I did not have any problem with swallowing.

"That was lovely," said Auntie Edie, "Sing another one."

I sang 'Silent Night' and While Shepherds Watched', and ended with 'Good King Wenceslas'. We had sung these at school and I had sung the part of the page boy. When I sang it for Uncle and Auntie, I tried to make a difference between the King's voice and the page, and I sang

Hither page and stand by me .....

in a strong voice, changing to a quieter, clear voice when the page replied

Sire, the night is darker now .....

They smiled and applauded, and said how much they had enjoyed our Christmas concert. We finished our celebrations with Auntie's Christmas cake and hot mince pies.

"You're quite a big girl now, I think you can have a

117

Christmas drink," they said, and they poured me a glass of Stone's Green Ginger wine. It was the first time I had ever had an alcoholic drink. I did not really like it – I thought it was quite strong and rather hot, but I felt very grown-up and drank it all.

'Stone's Green Ginger wine' is still available to this day with the same label on the bottle, and I cannot drink it without being transported to my wartime Christmas with that wonderful couple.

THE SCHOLARSHIP EXAMINATION

During the final year of junior school education, plans had to be made for transfer to a senior school. In the spring of 1943, just before my eleventh birthday, I was to sit the 'Scholarship Examination', a pre-runner of the eleven-plus. There were no other pupils in the school in my year group, so I was the only candidate.

Mrs Peacock's infants' class joined the juniors in the big classroom, and a desk and chair were put in the infants' room for me.

The examination started with twenty-five mental arithmetic questions. Miss Reddall read them slowly, repeating each question in case I had not heard it properly. She waited quite a long time between questions, so that I had plenty of time to work them out.

The next paper was 'Problems'. These were more difficult than the mental arithmetic questions, and you could not work them out in your head. At the top of the page, it said 'Show your working'.

One of the questions was similar to a problem that we had done with Miss Reddall in class:

Every day from a spring
A boy had to bring
Two gallons in a twenty-ounce pot
If a pint of clear water
Weighs a pound and a quarter
What weight had the little boy got?

You needed to know that there are eight pints in a gallon, and that there are sixteen ounces in a pound. When you had worked out the weight of the water, it was important to remember to add on the weight of the pot. There was enough time in the scholarship exam to check all your answers when you had finished, in case you had made any mistakes, or missed anything out.

In the middle of the examination, the rest of the school went out to play and I could hear them in the playground, outside the window. I knew they would all be going to the toilet, and wondered if I would be allowed to go.

"Please may I be excused?" I asked. I did not really need to go, but I wanted to see my friends.

"You can go when playtime is finished," I was told, "when they all come back in."

The only door in the infants' room led into the junior class, so I would have to walk through their lesson to get to the playground – or so I thought. But in an examination, you are not allowed to be with other people, in case they tell you the answers. So when they were back in class, I had to climb out of the window into the playground, go to the toilet, and climb back in again.

Back to the examination, there were two parts to the English paper. First 'The Comprehension' where you had to read a story, and answer questions to show you had understood it, and then 'The Composition' where you would write your own story.

Finally, there was a 'General Knowledge' paper. Miss Reddall did not mark the papers herself, but she looked through them before she put them in the big brown envelope.

"Well done, June," she said, "You've got all of your mental arithmetic questions right!"

Now I would have to wait two or three months for the results to come through, which would determine which school I would be going to in September.

* * * * * * * * *

I was not at all concerned about the impending results of the examination. I did not appreciate its significance, and gave it little or no thought. I knew I was too old to stay with Miss Reddall for another year, and that I would have to move on, but they knew what was best, and when there is a war on, you just go where you are sent and make the best of it. The scholarship examination was over and I forgot all about it.

It was at the beginning of the summer term when Miss Reddall had something important to say to the class.

"Put down your pencils," she said, "and sit up straight." We sat up, waiting to hear what she had to say.

"You will remember that last term June sat the Scholarship exam. Well, I'm sure you will all be pleased to know that she has passed with flying colours, so let's congratulate her with a big round of applause."

They all looked at me and clapped. I felt very proud and important, and I was more pleased with their approval than with the actual results.

I felt extremely happy, not because of the favourable educational prospects that this result promised, but because of the recognition and acclaim I had received from my classmates. It was not until later that I realised that my days at Newnham School were coming to an end, and that I would be leaving Radwell, and Auntie Edie and Uncle 'erbert, to go I knew not where.

Miss Radwell explained that my results were in the top group and that I could apply for a place in a Grammar School. The results had been sent to my parents and they would choose the school, and make all the necessary arrangements.

It was Dad, of course, who made the choice. He was good at dealing with correspondence and filling in forms. The Skinners' Company's School for Girls seemed to have three influencing factors: it was evacuated to Welwyn Garden City in Hertfordshire, which sounded as though it was near Radwell; its London base was at Stamford Hill in North London, so I would be able to continue there when the war was over; and it was one of four schools linked to 'The Worshipful Company of Skinners', one of the 'Great Twelve' livery companies.

In retrospect, none of these advantages is very persuasive. Even though Welwyn Garden City was in Hertfordshire, it would involve moving and I could just as easily have moved to any other county; the journey from Holborn to Stamford Hill was over six miles and there was no direct public transport. It would entail a journey on the underground, followed by a bus-ride, a total travelling time of more than an hour, and there were Grammar Schools much closer to home. The final attraction, which I suspect greatly influenced my father, was the prestigious reputation of the Skinners' Company. It was an ancient City Company, with a history dating back over seven hundred years, with the impressive 'Skinners' Hall' in Dowgate Hill, rebuilt in the 17th century after the Great Fire of London.

There was much rivalry between the 'Great Twelve' City Companies and a generally accepted order of precedence. The undisputed leader was the Company of Mercers, followed in the next four places by Grocers, Drapers, Fishmongers and Goldsmiths. There was no agreement however, as to which Company came next with Skinners and Merchant Tailors both claiming sixth position. Since neither was prepared to concede, an order was made in 1484 by Alderman Billesden that the Companies alternate between sixth and seventh place each year, and it is believed that this arrangement is the origin of the well-known saying 'to be all at sixes and sevens'.

The fame and wealth of the Skinners' Company was built in the fur trade, and I held no strong views on the subject at that time. If my present views on the fur trade had surfaced during my school years, I would have found it very distressing. Fortunately I had no thoughts on the subject and I was always very proud of

the school and its reputation. In 1943, I was quite happy to accept decisions which were made.

When I saw the uniform list and the other requirements I was quite convinced that Dad had made a wise choice. I had never seen anybody wearing a school uniform. At Newnham, we could wear what we liked, and even the pupils who went to the Secondary school in Ashwell wore ordinary clothes. Now it seemed that everybody at Skinners' would be wearing black tunics with white square-necked blouses and V-necked jumpers with a red stripe round the neck. The black blazer with red stripes had the Skinners' Company coat-of-arms on the pocket, and was topped with a black velour hat in winter and a straw hat in summer. Our house shoes were to be black with a buttoned strap across the foot.

It wasn't just the clothes which impressed me. We needed a science overall, an apron, and a black woollen swimming costume. We would also be using some very exciting equipment for mathematics – a compass, a setsquare and a protractor.

There was a shop in London which stocked our uniform, and a trip to the city was arranged. We qualified for an annual grant of nine pounds a year which was paid in termly instalments, and of course, we had to use our limited supply of clothing coupons.

The new school term would begin in September after the long summer holiday, but there was a problem each year in finding accommodation. The girls in the three hostels had to be billeted in private homes to make room for the new intake, and I was advised to remain where I was until I was sent for. It was going to be a very long summer holiday.

* * * * * * * * *

The warm spring of 1943 was followed by a long hot summer. Everybody has a summer like that during childhood. It is the one which is fixed in the memory, and which influences our recall of childhood, when we claim in later years, 'We used to have wonderful summers when I was a child, long sunny days, with blue skies and never a drop of rain'.

It was idyllic. It was also very lonely, because by 1943, all the other evacuees had returned home, and none of the few local children was my own age. There was no one to play with, and there were only two places to go for companionship, the church and the farm.

All Saints Church – Radwell

On Sundays, it was always the church, for morning and evening service. I was in the choir, which, by 1943 was so depleted that I often had to lead in, which meant walking up the aisle, very, very slowly, and then between the choir stalls, before turning at the end, back towards the congregation to the first choir pew. It was obviously the most important place to sit.

One Sunday, my mother made one of her rare visits to Radwell to see me, and Grandma came with her. Obviously, I could not miss Morning Service, so they had to come with me. I really wanted them to see how grand I looked in the flowing purple robe with its pleated back and billowing sleeves, which were so wide that you could lift your arms and they would spread out like wings. This was worn with a matching four-cornered hat, and, of course, they would realise how important I was.

'We have to get there early', I explained, 'as I have to ring the bell', which was another way of saying 'If we get there before Joan, I'll be able to ring the bell, and you'll see how clever I am'. Mum and Grandma watched with admiration as I untied the rope from the hook on the wall, and started to get the heavy bell on the move. Bell ringing is very much a question of timing, knowing when to pull on the rope on its way down, and when to release it again. 'You have to grab hold of the sally as it comes down' I explained, knowing that they would not have heard of that word, used to describe the woolly bit on the rope, 'and if you hold on too long' I warned, 'you could be dragged up into the bell tower by the weight of the bell'. I thought they needed to know that it was a dangerous activity, as well as requiring my skilful timing.

The bell rang out across the village for four or five minutes, summoning the Faithful to worship, after which, I showed Mum and Grandma to their pew, near the front, where they would be able to see everything, but avoiding the pews which were normally occupied by the regulars. Sitting in one of those pews would be as bad as sitting in Dad's big chair – not to be highly recommended. I opened their prayer books at the beginning of 'Morning Prayer', and drew their attention to the hymn numbers on the board, as well as the psalm, and then left them to get on with it. It was too complicated to explain where they would find the Gospel reading, or the Collect for the Day. You needed to attend regularly if you wanted to follow the whole service, and it wouldn't matter if they missed a bit.

I returned to the back of the church, and put on my robe and hat. The congregation stood as the opening chords of the processional hymn were heard on the organ, and I led the choir up the aisle, majestically, like a queen approaching her coronation. I could see Mum and Grandma out of the corner of my eye, turning their heads towards me, but I looked straight ahead, fixing my pious gaze steadily on the altar. It was streaked with rainbow coloured light as the morning sun shone through the magnificent stained glass window and I ignored their admiring approval of my grandeur. They must have been impressed to see how confidently I followed the service, giving the lead on when to sit, kneel, stand or turn to face the altar. During the sermon I sat with my arms folded staring intently at the Reverend Baylay as though I were listening to every word he was saying, and being spiritually uplifted by his message. I was more concerned with not letting my eyes wander in case I met their gaze and was expected to acknowledge them with a little smile.

I maintained my impeccable performance throughout the service, and even during the retiring procession, which was quite difficult as we were almost face to face as I passed their pew, not more than two or three feet away.

On reaching the back of the church, when everyone else was disrobing, I returned to my normal self, and walked back to talk to them, still wearing my beautiful gown. 'That was a very nice service', said Mum, and Grandma smiled in agreement, and said 'Doesn't that colour suit her? And do you know', she added, 'I've always thought she looks like Vivien Leigh, with those high cheekbones'.

Vivien Leigh, the beautiful star of stage and screen was famous for her role as Scarlet O'Hara in *'Gone with the Wind'*, and the seductive Cleopatra, bewitching Julius Caesar and Mark Anthony with her flawless beauty. She was almost an icon in her time, her beauty being beyond question, being second only, perhaps to Elizabeth Taylor.

No one had ever spotted my resemblance to Vivien Leigh before – or since for that matter – but it must have been there as Grandma had seen it. It may have been enhanced by the magic of the rich purple robe, and there was no denying I certainly had the high cheekbones, but it needed a vivid imagination and a measure of wishful thinking on the part of a doting Grandma to make the connection.

DIG FOR VICTORY

The war had brought about an agricultural revolution. Imports from abroad were very limited, and only essential supplies were brought in. The Merchant Navy ships carrying these goods were escorted by Royal Navy destroyers, to protect them from enemy warships, but many were still lost by torpedo attacks from German submarines.

As far as was possible, the country had to be self-sufficient. Unused land was reclaimed, government grants were given and productivity was closely monitored. We were urged to 'Dig For Victory', and garden flowers and lawns gave way to vegetables. The Ministry of Food published cookery tips showing exciting ways of feeding a family on potatoes and carrots.

The war dragged on, and there was no end in sight. Much of the propaganda was aimed at housewives on the 'Kitchen Front' and by encouraging them to believe that they were making a positive and important 'war effort', spirits could be lifted and

morale raised. Patriotic films, such as Noel Coward's 'In Which We Serve', and news documentaries kept our minds focused on the honourable purpose of the conflict. We were all fighting this war, we were in it together, and together we were going to win.

The introduction of *'Double British Summer Time'* maximised the use of daylight hours, so that harvesting could continue late into the evening. Horses gave way to tractors, which during the course of the war increased in number from 50,000 to 200,000, and the novelty of these new machines, and the speed with which they worked, helped to raise morale. A circular from the Ministry of Agriculture *'Plough by Day and Night'* urged farmers to fit lights to tractors, and not surprisingly food production doubled. The importance of farming was recognised by all and there was a new sense of pride down on the farm.

In May 1943 war work became compulsory for women aged 18 to 50 years and only mothers with young children and the disabled were exempt. Many joined the uniformed services: the Auxiliary Territorial Service (A.T.S), the Women's Royal Naval Service (W.R.N.S), or the

Her Royal Highness, Princess Elizabeth

Women's Auxiliary Air Force (W.A.A.F). They worked as radio operators, ambulance drivers, nurses, etc, but were not allowed to fight in battle. Even Princess Elizabeth at the age of eighteen, was put into A.T.S uniform and photographed in front of her army truck, which interestingly carried a red 'L' plate. She was seen by all to be 'doing her bit'.

Those who were not attracted to the uniformed services were directed to other essential employment, to *'Work of National Importance'* working in the munitions factories, driving buses, nursing, balloon operating or cooking in mobile canteens. Many at this time were conscripted to the Women's Land Army, joining those who had been recruited voluntarily in 1939, and they were able to do most, if not all the work previously done by the men.

Additional labour on the farm was sometimes provided by Italian Prisoners of War, always referred to as 'Ities'. They were based at a camp in the area, and were trucked in by their guards to whichever farm had the greatest need, and they could easily be identified by their blue and white striped shirts.

I think they were always given the worst jobs, because I only ever saw them potato-picking which was very boring, and made your back ache. That was fair, really, because they were on Hitler's side in the war, so we didn't have to give them the best jobs. Their contribution to the work at harvest time was appreciated but there was considerable resentment towards them. They were unlikely to try to escape, it was argued, because they had a 'cushy life', comfortable and safe, whilst 'our boys' were living in danger, and no-one could be certain that

> *'Jimmy would go to sleep,*
> *In his own little room again'.*

The farmers were responding to the government appeal to *'Dig for Victory'* and there was a sense of urgency on the farm. Willing hands were always welcome. I started off just hanging around, but soon made myself useful by running errands or going back to collect someone's forgotten sandwiches. After a while I began to do more useful things, like making sure that the bull had enough water in his trough. He was very big and dangerous, and had a ring through his nose, and he was kept locked up. If his water trough was dry, I had to fill the bucket by dipping it in the big tank and pouring the water through a small hole in the wall. I think he would have preferred to have been out in the field with the cows, but he was too dangerous.

Bringing the cows in at milking time was quite easy because they were always waiting at the gate. All you had to do was open the gate and they went into the cowshed on their own. They even knew their own places. 'We'll make a cowgirl out of you' said Mr Wyant, 'but you'll have to be here at six o'clock in the morning for the first milking'. I did not think that was a very good idea, because with *'Double British Summertime'*, all our clocks were two hours fast, and it was still dark at six o'clock. I didn't mind making my 'war effort' for the evening milking.

To milk a cow, you had to sit on a stool with a bucket under the heavy udders with the top of your head leaning against the side of the cow, and squirt the milk into the bucket. The milk came out in a very fast jet, and you could squirt it over somebody for a joke, like a water pistol. At least, you could, if you knew how to do it, but I could never get the hang of it. I squeezed the teats and I pulled them; I tried stroking them and jerking them but I never once succeeded in getting a steady stream of milk into the bucket. The best I could get was a few slow drips. I was never going to be a cowgirl. I was disappointed but there were other things I could do to help.

I knew I wasn't really supposed to be there, and the foreman said to me, 'You'd better not let Mr Walker see you working here. If you see him coming, you'd better make yourself scarce'. But Mr Walker, the farmer, knew what was going on, and once when he came round and saw me standing there, I heard him say, 'Is she all right? Keep an eye on her – we don't want any accidents' and the foreman replied, 'Yes sir, she is fine, and I'm keeping an eye on her'.

The work I enjoyed most on the farm was harvesting when I could ride on the tractor, or on the hay cart. When we were cutting the corn, we had the harvester behind the tractor, which would cut the wheat, barley or oats, tie it into sheaves, and throw them out on to the field. Then we had to take 4 or 5 sheaves and stand them up, leaning one against another like a wigwam, so that they could dry in the sun.

About a week later, we would collect them on the hay cart and take them back to the farm to build a haystack. This was very hard work and I was not big enough. The farm labourers had to dig their pitchforks into the sheaves and toss them up onto the cart, where one man had to arrange them neatly so that they would not fall off. This was when I was allowed to drive the tractor. Well, it wasn't really driving. I just had to keep it going in a straight line. There was one big foot pedal, and I had to lift it slowly to make the tractor go. When the hay cart was next to a wigwam I had to push the pedal down again to stop the tractor, and keep it down until they had tossed the sheaves on to the cart. When we got to the end of the row one of the men would turn the tractor round ready for me to drive it back along the next row. With an extra man pitching, it did not take us so long to load the cart and get it back to the farm. I think Mr Walker must have been quite pleased.

One day in particular stands out in my memory, when we were cutting wheat in the top field. We used to start by going round the edge of the field, following the line of the hedges, and moving inwards on each circuit. There were always rabbits in the corn and they would run away from the noisy tractor. Occasionally, you would see one making a dash for safety, running across the stubble to the hedges. There were always one or two rabbits that thought they could hide in the corn, but as we went round and round, their hiding place was gradually disappearing, and, sooner or later they would have to make a bid for safety across the open field. When there was not much corn left standing, we stopped the tractor and took out the sticks which were carried for that purpose. We spread ourselves around the corn hoping to catch a rabbit on its way out, 'You'll have to be very fast,' said one of the farm labourers, 'and you'll have to hit it hard!' That didn't seem to be a problem. I was the fastest runner in the school, and I was very strong for a girl. Then one of the men, with a big beer-belly called out to the men on each side of me, 'Get in a bit closer to the girl – she'll never catch it!' 'What a cheek,' I thought, 'I bet he can't move very fast, he's too fat. I'll show him, I'll surprise him'.

This was going to be good. I could imagine myself carrying the rabbit home, holding it by its back legs, nonchalantly thrown over my shoulder. Auntie Edie would be amazed. 'What's that you've got there?' she would ask in disbelief. 'Oh, it's just a rabbit I caught up in the top field,' I would explain, modestly, 'I thought you might be able to make a rabbit pie'.

Now, of course, meat was strictly rationed. We were allowed only about one shilling's worth of meat for each person each week. The amount would vary from month to month according to availability. Every month, there was a government announcement giving the value of the coupons for the following month.

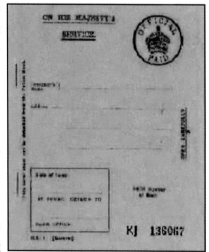

World War II Ration Book

Meat was different from the other rationed items as the amount allowed was determined by price, not weight. Twelve ounces of sugar would always be the same, but meat varied in quality and some cuts had more gristle and fat, and more waste. If you bought the cheaper cuts you would get more for your money. You could not shop around for the best bargains, because you had to register with a retailer, who would have only enough meat for his own customers. You could not save your coupons and use them in the following month, or even the following week, so the shopkeepers always knew exactly what the demand would be for each week.

You could, if you wanted, give the whole page of coupons to the retailer, who then had to sign your book, but if you were likely to want to buy a meat meal in a café or restaurant, you would need half a coupon which is why the meat coupons had a line across the middle.

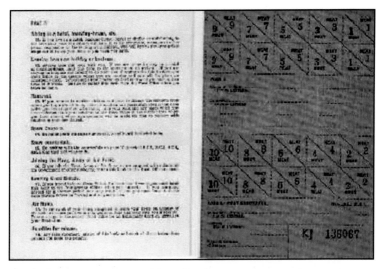

Meat Coupons

Sausages were not rationed, but they were always in short supply. A free rabbit would be a real treat, a bonus! All I had to do was to catch one. It was easier for the farmers, because they had guns. Sometimes, you could hear the gunshots across the fields. We used to sing

> *'Run rabbit, run rabbit, run, run, run*
> *Here comes the farmer with his gun, gun, gun,*
> *He'll get by, without his rabbit pie*
> *So run, rabbit, run rabbit, run, run, run'.*

Well, I would have to catch mine with my stick. When Uncle 'erbert came home from work he would smell the pie in the oven as he opened the door, and he would ask 'What's cooking?' and Auntie Edie would tell him. I wanted to impress them both, and I wanted to prove to beer-belly how good I was. All I wanted was the opportunity. I prayed that there would be at least one rabbit still in the corn. If there were any, they wouldn't run towards the noisy tractor. "Are you ready?" asked the man. I was ready. I could feel my heart pounding and the adrenalin flowing. I was very still and alert, like a sprinter at the start of a race, waiting for the gun. I was holding my stick shoulder height ready to strike. 'Oh please, let there be a rabbit in the corn,' I prayed, 'and please, please let it come out nearest to me'.

The man started to wade through the corn towards us, shouting loudly, and thrashing the corn with his stick. I waited, every muscle tense, watching the corn for a sign of movement. My prayers were answered. A rabbit appeared from the corn just in front of me and ran towards me. I felt myself relax and I lowered my stick. 'Oh, isn't he sweet?' I said as he ran past me, not more than four or five feet away, the perfect hitting distance, and I know I could have got him. I watched him, his little white tail bobbing as he crossed the field to the safety of the hedges.

'He'll be so happy to get back home to his family,' I thought. That was not what beer-belly thought, and he swore with anger. He was not impressed, but I think St Francis must have been proud of me, and I was very happy.

When I got home, I wanted to tell Auntie Edie and Uncle 'erbert what had happened and I wondered if they would have been pleased to know that I had been so kind to the rabbit but I was scared to tell them in case they were too disappointed at not getting their rabbit pie.

I thought of this incident many times afterwards because I had learned a very valuable lesson. You may think you know how you are going to react to a situation, but until it actually happens, you don't know what you will do.

* * * * * * * *

The long summer holidays came to an end and the local children went back to school. I was ready to leave Radwell and move to Welwyn Garden City to join '*The Skinners' Company's Grammar School for Girls*', but I had been told to 'stay where you are until you are sent for'. Every September with the fresh intake of pupils they had to find new billets in the town, and this might take a few weeks. Now, the harvesting was finished and the work on the farm was not so interesting.

At Church, we had the 'Harvest Festival' and All Saints Church was filled with all the things that had been grown on the farm or in the gardens. You could see it had been a really good 'Dig for Victory' war effort. There were all kinds of vegetables – potatoes, carrots, parsnips, all without a trace of dirt. There were enormous marrows, shiny apples and plums, and bowls of currants, raspberries and gooseberries. Some of the ladies in the village had baked bread, which was plaited into fancy shapes, and of course, our sheaves of corn were there to be admired by all.

We sang the harvest hymns, 'We plough the fields and scatter' and 'Come ye thankful people come'

> *'All is safely gathered in'*
> *'Ere the winter storms begin'*

That hymn ended with:

> *'Come ye thankful people come'*
> *'Raise the song of harvest home'*

but I went home singing

> *'Run you lucky rabbit run'*
> *O'er the field and safely home'.*

October came, and there was still no letter summoning me to my new school. The other children envied me, having such a long summer holiday, and I pretended it was wonderful, but really it was beginning to be quite boring.

Sometimes I went into Baldock, where Uncle 'erbert worked in Simpson's Brewery. He used to fill the big barrels with beer and then hammer the bung into the hole. Then he had to roll the heavy barrels into the middle of the floor on to the iron 'tramlines'. This made it easier to trundle them along to the other end near the door where they would be loaded on to the lorries. I think it was very hard work and there was a very unpleasant smell of beer, but Uncle 'erbert never complained about anything. He was always very cheerful, and I knew I would miss him very much when I left Radwell.

There was a cinema in Baldock, and I went there sometimes. My favourite film was *'Sun Valley Serenade'* with Sonja Henie. She was very famous because she had won lots of medals for ice-skating and skiing in the Winter Olympic Games before the war. She was also very pretty, and now that we were not having any Olympic Games, she decided to be a film star instead.

In this film she was a refugee, which is like an evacuee and she was going to be billeted with John Payne. He was expecting her to be a little girl, like I was when I went to Radwell, so when he went to meet her at the station he had bought her a teddy bear. I thought that was very funny. He already had a girlfriend who was not very good at skiing, and, because Sonja Henie was so good at skiing and skating, and very pretty, he fell in love with her instead.

For me, the film was a revelation and an education. I did not know that mountains could be so high, or that there could be so much snow. You could ride up the mountains in a gondola or on a chair lift so that you could fly down again on skis. I remembered how exciting it had been when we went tobogganing in the dell, two years earlier, even though we didn't get a very long ride down and we had to drag our toboggans back up to the top again. It had been great fun but this……. this was different, and it was exciting just to watch it. The scenery was breathtakingly beautiful and there were even Christmas trees growing on the mountain slopes, with the branches decorated with snow. It was a new world and it was like being in fairyland. I was completely captivated by Sonja Henie, and her skiing left me spellbound. She was very graceful and she made it all look so easy. I hoped that one day I would be able to find the mountains and learn to ski.

With time hanging heavily on my hands, I went to see

this programme twice. With it, there was a supporting film, which also made an impression on me but for quite a different reason. It was an American film that I did not really understand. There was a woman who was always quarrelling with her husband. 'I want a divorce!' she shouted, and she filled in a form to send to her solicitor. As she put the envelope in the post-box she said, 'There, now I shall get a divorce!' I had not heard that word before, and I was intrigued to know what it was that she wanted so much. Auntie Edie would know.

'What's a divorce?' I asked, when I got home. 'Oh', she said slowly, 'you don't want to bother yourself about words like that'. Dear Auntie Edie – she probably wondered if Mum and Dad were having problems, and didn't want me to be worried. It would not have been surprising. The anxiety of the war and long periods of separation put a strain on relationships. Mum was evacuated most of the time. Billets were found for mothers with young children but they didn't always last long. It must have been very difficult living in someone else's home with a toddler. There was even a film, made by the Government in 1941, called *'Living with Strangers'* which made helpful suggestions to mothers with young children and the host families on things like sharing the kitchen. Needless to say there were bound to be problems and Mum never stayed for long in the same place. She stayed in various billets in the Letchworth and Hitchin areas leaving Dad at home alone for most of the time. He was not very good at looking after himself and didn't do the washing-up very often. He would just take a clean cup and plate out of the cupboard every time he needed one. When he knew Mum was coming home he would do the washing up before she arrived. On one occasion, Dad had not received

Mum's letter so he was not expecting her, and she was amazed to find that he had started using the Best Tea Service which was never used, because it was a wedding present.

I can understand why Auntie Edie may have wondered if their marriage was going to survive the war. So many people were being killed and no one could be sure that they would ever be re-united with their families. With young men going off to war, perhaps never to return, there was a general feeling of 'living for the day'. Auntie Edie need not have worried about Mum and Dad, but she was doing her best, as she always did, to protect me. She was a wonderful lady.

* * * * * * * * *

The days dragged on, and still there was no letter from my new school. I wandered aimlessly down the lane stopping from time to time to eat a few blackberries. Then I had an idea. A blackberry and apple pie would compensate for not having had our rabbit pie.

I went back to the house, and when Auntie Edie wasn't looking I took a very big bowl from the cupboard and made my way to a field where I knew there would be a good picking. The best ones were always just out of reach and even with the help of a stick to pull the branches down, you ended up with scratches on your arms and legs. Usually, you ate the best ones straight away, but not this time. The best were for Auntie Edie and Uncle 'erbert, and if I could ever fill this bowl, there would be enough left over to make blackberry and apple jam as well. I picked for hours, my fingers blue with the stain from blackberry juice and the backs of my hands bleeding, until the bowl was filled to the top.

Auntie Edie was delighted. 'I'll make a pie', she said predictably, 'and tomorrow, I'll bottle some for the winter, and make some jam'. I peeled and cored the apples from the garden while she made the pastry. Auntie Edie served the pie at dinner with hot custard. 'Which do you like best?' I asked them. 'Blackberry and apple pie or rabbit pie?' Uncle 'erbert could see the scratches on my hands. 'Oh, definitely, blackberry and apple pie,' he said, giving the right answer, without understanding the significance of the question, and Auntie Edie agreed.

It was worth having all those scratches to hear them say that, and I felt vindicated for failing to bring home the rabbit.

JOCK

The autumn leaves turned to gold, and started to fall, and this was the best time of the year to collect nuts. You had to know the difference between sweet chestnut trees, which had nuts you could roast and eat, and horse chestnut trees which had conkers. I don't think you could give them to horses. It's no good collecting the best conkers if you've got no one to play with. I gave some of mine away, but not the best ones. I really had enough, but with nothing better to do, I wandered down to the woods again and collected a few more.

On my way back I stopped to talk to the soldier on guard outside The White House. I think the house was really called Radwell Manor, but we always called it the White House because the building next to the lane was painted white. This was where the stables used to be, but it was now used as a guardroom.

There was always a guard on duty, who carried a gun. Guards were very important and were not supposed to talk to anyone while they were on duty. They had to make sure that there were no spies trying to get into their camp, but they were usually very friendly and would talk to you if no one was looking. They were always on the look out for a car on its way out, or coming back down the lane. Anyone in a car was obviously very important – a Major or a Colonel, and the guard immediately jumped to attention and saluted as the car went by.

Today, it was Jock who was on duty. He was from Scotland, and had a very strong accent. 'I've found some very big conkers' I said, showing them to him. 'I think this will be a good one' he said, taking one from the bag. He threw it up into the air, and tried to head it as it came down. He wasn't looking out for cars that he might have to salute on their way in or out. 'Where is everybody?' I asked, looking through the gate to the empty drill yard. The place looked deserted. 'They're away off on manoeuvres' he replied. 'I'm in charge now. Did I no see you in the concert?' He asked 'I saw ye standing on your head'. 'Yes,' I replied with pride. 'I was the acrobat, and I was in the chorus as well. Did you see me singing? I was near the end of the line.' 'Aye' he said, 'I saw ye, and ye were a very good acrobat. Would ye no like a cup of tea?'

he asked. 'I don't drink tea,' I replied, 'I'd rather have orange juice or water'. 'I'll see what I have,' he said, 'come this way lassie'.

The White House

I followed him in amazement. I couldn't believe that after four years I was actually going into the barracks. For four years I'd stood outside wondering what it was like beyond the gate. It was like standing outside Buckingham Palace – you could press your face against the railings and try to imagine what it was like inside, but you knew you would never go in. And here I was following Jock into the guardroom. It was not at all as I expected it to be. It was a small room with white walls and with a very high window. There was not much furniture – a wooden table and some chairs. There was a teapot on the table, and some cups which did not look very clean. 'Would ye be liking a biscuit?' asked Jock.

'I like those!' I said, pointing to the custard creams and he pushed the packet across the table saying, 'Help yourself lassie'. Then he said, 'Would ye like me to draw your portrait?' I knew that a portrait was a picture of a person, or sometimes just the face.

If it was a man it was usually because he was very important, like a king or a famous soldier in uniform, and if it was a lady it was because she was very pretty. 'Yes please' I replied.

He turned the chairs round, so that we were facing each other, and took a big pad out of the drawer. I knew I had to sit very still, like when you have a photograph taken, but this would take a lot longer. He started drawing with a black stick, which was charcoal. He kept looking up at me while he was drawing, but I couldn't see the portrait. He stopped drawing and rubbed the paper with his finger, and I wondered if he had made a mistake, and if it would look smudged. Then he carried on drawing. He stopped, and pulled his chair up a bit closer, and leaned forward so that he could get a better view, and he rested his other hand on the edge of my chair, between my knees. I didn't know if I should smile a little bit, like you do for a photo, but it's hard to keep a smile on all the time. I wondered if he would see the resemblance to Vivien Leigh. Now that he was leaning forward, I could see the portrait but I couldn't tell if I looked like her as it was upside down. I watched him drawing my eyebrows and, again, he rubbed it with his finger. 'Why do you rub it?' I asked, hoping they were not mistakes. 'It makes it look better' he explained, 'If you blur the lines a wee bit, it gives it a softer look,' I felt relieved, and thought it would be very good.

I was sitting very still. Jock was concentrating hard on his work and I thought he must not have realised that his hand was slowly slipping towards me on the wooden chair. It was because he was leaning forward. I didn't say anything because he was too busy with his drawing and I didn't want to interrupt him. He was shading the side of my nose and one eye, and his hand slipped a bit more on the chair. Then he started drawing my mouth and I wondered if I should try to smile again. He rubbed the corner of my mouth with his finger, and his hand slipped again. I did not move. The portrait looked very good, upside-down. I could see that one ear was partly covered by my hair, and that one side of my face was nearly done. I was very eager to see the finished portrait, but I would have to be patient a bit longer. Jock was so engrossed in his work that he could not have realised that his hand had slipped a bit more and that his knuckles were now pressing against my knickers. I sat very, very still and could not disturb him in case it spoiled the portrait, and he carried on with his drawing. Then I felt a little movement as one finger gently pulled aside the elastic in my knickers. I immediately tipped my chair backwards on to two legs, and jumped off the chair saying, 'I think I'd better go now – it's getting late, and Auntie Edie said I must not be late'.

I didn't stop to look at the portrait or even pick up my conkers. I left the guardroom, and the barracks and ran back up the lane to Auntie Edie. I wanted to tell her what had happened but I thought I might get into trouble. I knew I wasn't supposed to go into the guardroom, and I hadn't stopped Jock when his hand kept slipping – so it was really my own fault.

I decided not to say anything but I felt really upset because everything seemed to have gone wrong. I didn't like Jock anymore so I didn't want to see him again; that meant I wouldn't be able to get my conkers back; and I hadn't seen the portrait so I still didn't know if I looked like Vivien Leigh!

LEAVING RADWELL

'You never forget people who were kind to you when you were young'   The Observer – Sayings of the Eighties – Mark Birley

At last, the letter from my new school arrived. I was to join them at the end of October, in the half term holiday, having missed seven weeks' schooling. I was excited and very nervous. I had been looking forward to this move for so long, and now that it was upon me, and I had no choice, I didn't really want to go.

I knew the school would be very different from Miss Reddall's village school in Newnham. You could tell that from the uniform list. There was the black blazer with red stripes, with the school badge and motto: - *'Honour Before Honours, To God Only Be All Glory',* and the hats; black velour in the winter and a straw hat in summer. And there were all the other things; a science overall, a cookery apron, PT kit, a black regulation swimming costume and all the mathematics equipment. I could not imagine using all these things, and it was certainly going to be very different. I wouldn't know anybody there and at the end of the school day I would not be coming home to Auntie Edie and Uncle 'erbert. I wondered who I would be living with, and if I would like them, and if they would like me. The more I thought about it, the less I wanted to go, but – it had all been arranged. You had to change schools when you were eleven years old, and I had to go.

My bag was packed and I had to catch the Baldock bus at the top of the road at ten o'clock, and get a train to Welwyn Garden City, and Mum would be there to meet me at the station.

I thought of what Auntie Edie had said at Christmas when I had sung the Christmas carols to them. 'We did not want to have an evacuee at the beginning of the war,' she said, 'We thought we were too old, but you have made us feel young again'. I hoped they would still feel young when I had gone.

The day of departure arrived, my suitcase was packed and I was ready to leave. I had to say goodbye to Auntie Edie and Uncle 'erbert and, of course, to Trixie. "I wish I could take Trixie with me." I said as I cuddled and stroked her.

"I think she would like some chocolate buttons before you go," said Uncle 'erbert, "Why don't you give her a few? I think she knows you are leaving." I took the box from the cupboard and rattled it, and she jumped on to the chair as she always did, and stood up with her paws on the back of the chair.

"This is my goodbye present!," I said, as she swallowed the chocolates without chewing them, "Because I've got to go away to a new school." And then I gave her a last cuddle. I kissed Auntie Edie and Uncle 'erbert and they both gave me a big hug.

"We'll miss you." said Uncle 'erbert, as he carried my bag out for me, and they both stood at the gate to watch me go.

Every few yards, I stopped and turned to wave goodbye to them, past the village hall where I had first seen Auntie Edie, past the dell where I had tobogganed, past the meadow where I had teased the grasshoppers and made them jump, until finally after my last wave they disappeared from my view as I turned the bend in the lane. And I never saw them again – I never spoke to them – I never even wrote to them. I walked out of their lives, as I had walked in four years earlier. For all they knew, I might have been killed by a bomb.

I did try to write from the dormitory of the school hostel. I knew how to write a letter – we had done that with Miss Reddall. You put the address at the top right hand corner, with the commas in the right place, and then the date, and then you started a bit lower down on the left with 'Dear So-and-So,' not forgetting another comma. It was not really difficult, but there was a lot to remember if you wanted to get it right, and I think this was to be my first real letter.

'Dear Auntie Edie and Uncle 'erbert, I am sorry I have not written before but I have been very busy'. I didn't know what to say next, and I didn't like the first sentence – too busy to write to Auntie Edie and Uncle 'erbert? I tore it up. A few days later, I tried again. 'Dear Uncle 'erbert and Auntie Edie, I go to a very big school now, and I am learning to speak French.' That wasn't right either. They were simple country folk, and speaking French could only put a barrier between us, so I tore that one up too. A few weeks later, I tried again. 'Dear Uncle 'erbert and Auntie Edie, I hope you are well. You'd hardly recognise me now, as I wear my hair in plaits'…..That had to go in the bin. I didn't want them to think I had changed, but I could not find the right words because the right words don't come easily. What I really wanted to say was, 'Thank you, and I love you, and I miss you very much'.

When the war was over, I went back to see them, but I was too late. Auntie Edie had died and Uncle 'erbert had gone to live with his son 'Wags' in the Midlands. Oh, if only I had written that letter! If only Mum had been there, or a caring teacher who might have told me not to worry about getting the letter right, but to get it in the post. If only I had tried to trace Uncle 'erbert with his son – I think it might have been Nottingham – by going there, and searching through the electoral role.

Now, when I hear other evacuees, recounting their experiences, and describing the lasting bonds that were made with their foster-parents, the pain comes back, as it has done always throughout my life. I hear of foster-parents who were guests-of-honour at weddings. There have been return visits for holidays, shared joy at Christening celebrations, and an extra pair of adopted grandparents for the evacuee's children. I cannot begin to describe the anguish that my neglect has caused me over the years, - the regret, the sadness, the remorse I have felt so deeply for so long; the guilt I feel for the hurt and pain I must have caused them. They opened their home to me, and their hearts. They cared for me and loved me and I abandoned them.

I wonder how long it was before they realised that they were not going to hear from me again? Did they still talk about me? Or did I become one of those events about which one cannot speak because it is too painful, like the untimely death of a child?

Many years later, I found their grave in the churchyard, over by the fence. Auntie Edie had died in April 1944, aged 64, only six months after I left. In a strange way, this lightens my burden a little, knowing that she would not have been sure that I had gone for good, and I doubt if Uncle 'erbert expected to hear from me after he left Radwell even though he lived for another eighteen years. These small comforting thoughts cannot erase the heartache and torment of the years, but they do help.

During the war, Uncle and Auntie had received a *'Personal Message'* from Her Majesty Queen Elizabeth, in beautiful lettering, headed by a large and colourful Royal Crest. In it the Queen expressed appreciation to foster parents for opening their doors in 1939, to strangers who were in need of shelter, and for sharing their homes with them. They treasured this Royal Message, but I believe they would have traded it for a badly written letter from me, in which they would have been able to look beyond my inadequate choice of words to see an expression of my love and gratitude, and it would have enabled us to keep in touch throughout the years.

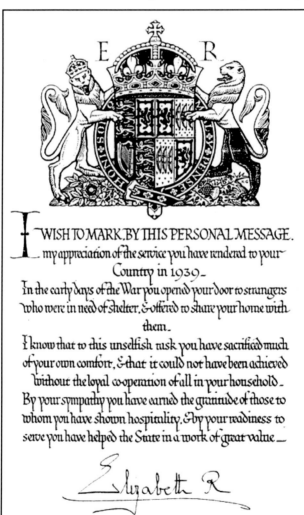

E R

I WISH TO MARK, BY THIS PERSONAL MESSAGE, my appreciation of the service you have rendered to your Country in 1939.

In the early days of the War you opened your door to strangers who were in need of shelter, & offered to share your home with them.

I know that to this unselfish task you have sacrificed much of your own comfort, & that it could not have been achieved without the loyal co-operation of all in your household. By your sympathy you have earned the gratitude of those to whom you have shown hospitality, & by your readiness to serve you have helped the State in a work of great value.

Elizabeth R

PART FOUR

'Welwyn Garden City 1943 to 1945'

'.....on the shore of the wide world, I stand alone.....'
                    John Keats - THE HOSTEL

Mum met me at the station and the ticket collector pointed us in the right direction. Welwyn Garden City was a 'new town' similar in many ways to Letchworth where Mum had been billeted. She carried one of my bags, and we followed our map along wide tree-lined roads with grass verges and green open spaces. Twenty-One Valley Road was one of three big houses in the town which had been requisitioned for use as hostel accommodation for evacuees. It was a big detached house with a large garage. The red brick walls were partly covered by a creeper and the trees in the garden were shedding their autumn leaves.

Twenty-One Valley Road

I rang the bell and waited. "Don't bite your nails," said Mum, and I quickly took my fingers out of my mouth. The door was opened by a young girl, not much more than seven or eight years old, who looked at me briefly, with my suitcase and turned, shouting, "The new girl's here." A lady came to the door, the warden, followed by an older girl. "June Matthews?" enquired the warden, inviting us in. "Yes", I replied, following her into the hall.

I was feeling very nervous and apprehensive and had butterflies in my stomach. I could see that Mum was feeling anxious, too. She was trying to smile, but it didn't look natural. "I'll be all right," I assured her, and she kissed me goodbye. "We'll look after her," said the Warden, "and Mavis will take June to her dormitory." Mum kissed me again and said, "Be a good girl," and I waved to her as I watched her go.

"You'll be in the same dormitory as Mavis," said the warden, "and she'll show you the ropes."

I was going to sleep in a dormitory! I knew that word because Mum had bought me a book for Christmas, called *'The Naughtiest Girl in the School'*, by Enid Blyton. It was about a girl called Elizabeth Allen, who went to a boarding school, and they had dormitories. Elizabeth was always up to mischief, and constantly in trouble, and everybody loved her. There were always pranks in the dormitory – apple-pie beds, midnight feasts, climbing out of windows, and so on, and I wondered if we would be having fun like that. Certainly, the idea appealed to me.

I followed Mavis up the stairs. She was a big girl with a friendly manner. She was a lot taller and heavier than I was and seemed to be much older, and I was surprised to find that we were almost exactly the same age.

"All of us in 'Big Dorm' are Third Formers," she explained as I followed her to our room. 'Big Dorm' was a long room with windows on two sides. There were six beds in a row, separated by bedside lockers.

"You're in the corner, next to Billie," said Mavis, "but she's gone home for the week-end, and won't be back till Sunday night."

"Can we go home for week-ends?" I asked hopefully.

"You have to get a pass," explained Mavis, "and you can only go once or twice in a term."

I wondered how much the fare would be, and whether Mum would be able to afford it. I was much nearer to London now, and Mum seemed to be back home for much of the time. If I didn't like it here it would not be too bad if I could go home sometimes. It would be something to look forward to.

I put my things on the bed, which looked very narrow, compared to the big bed I had got used to in Radwell. "They look very small," I said, and Mavis explained that they were army camp beds.

"You'll find it comfortable if you're small and like sleeping on a board! We've made your bed for you this time, because you're new, but next time, you'll have to do it yourself – and you'll have to look at the rota to see which day you have to strip your bed and put your dirty linen out."

I thanked her and looked round the dormitory. It was quite a bare room with brown lino on the floor and plain heavy blackout curtains. The blankets were dark grey and there was no colour in the room. It was really quite drab, and not at all homely, but it had one magnificent redeeming feature – one that would change my life. There was a washbasin, with two taps. I had never before lived in a house which had a tap.

In London, we had to fill the big enamel jug at the sink on the public landing and carry the water into the flat. It was carried out again in the slop bucket to be emptied down the lavatory. In Radwell, in the Farm Cottages, we had to wind the bucket up from the well, and in the Council Cottages, the water was drawn from the pump. Here, all you had to do was turn on the tap and out it came. And not just cold water, but hot as well. No more kettles on the gas, or saucepans on the copper, just turn on the tap and there it was! Then, there was the bathroom. Another washbasin with taps, and a big bath with more taps and, best of all, a flushing toilet!

This was another new experience. This was the first time I'd lived in a house with an indoor toilet. This was going to be better than going out to the public lavatory on the landing in Peabody Buildings; and there would be no smelly buckets to be emptied down the garden, like in Radwell. When you needed to go to the toilet, it was not far to walk, and afterwards all you had to do was pull the chain. I thought I would enjoy living in Valley Road.

Mavis showed me the notice board, and told me I should read the House Rules and the rotas. Each dormitory had a bedtime and a lights-out time, and there was a rota for the bath. There was a dormitory above the garage which must have been added as an extension because the only access to it was through the bathroom, so the senior girls, in 'Garage Dorm' had no access to their room when the bathroom was occupied. Time was rationed in the bathroom, and, of course, so was bathwater. The 'five inches of bathwater' rule which we had followed in Radwell was very strictly observed here.

Nobody would check, of course, but we all wanted to help, and by following this rule we could all feel that we were 'doing our bit'. I still didn't understand how having a shallow bath could make a difference. Nobody explained it to me, and I didn't ask. I just accepted it without question. Now – five inches of hot water, straight from the tap would be wonderful.

In London we had only the small zinc bath which we used to put in front of the fire and I was probably too big now to sit in that again. In Radwell, we had to carry the hot water from the copper boiler to the bathroom in a huge saucepan, and this meant quite a few journeys, so I didn't have a bath very often, and there was certainly no chance of having more than five inches. Life in Welwyn Garden City was going to be very different, quite luxurious.

Mavis explained the duty rota to me. "You have to do a duty every week," she explained, "and the list goes up at the weekend. If you're on 'potatoes' you have to peel them after dinner, ready for the next day. For most of the duties, you'll be working with someone else, so they'll tell you what to do. The easiest duty is 'laying'. You have to lay the tables for dinner, and then afterwards, wipe them down, and lay them ready for breakfast next morning. But we hardly ever get that one. They usually give it to the little ones in 'Pets Dorm'. Lower School don't stay up late enough to do 'Blackout and coals' or 'Washing-up'."

"What's Lower School?" I asked, a little surprised.

"The little ones in First Form, Second Form and Lower Three," explained Mavis, "they're only seven to ten years old, like Adrienne Jonas who opened the door to you."

"But I didn't think you could take the scholarship before you were eleven," I said.

"They haven't won a scholarship," said Mavis, "they're fee payers. Most of the pupils in this school pay fees. To come to this school you've got to be rich or brainy." I thought all schools were free, and that if I hadn't done well in the scholarship exam, I would have gone to the secondary school in Ashwell – and you wouldn't have to pay to go there. I didn't really know what the word 'scholarship' meant and I had just assumed that it was a test to determine the most suitable school. I hadn't realised that a scholarship involved money, and that someone – my Local Education Authority – would have to pay for me to go to this prestigious school. No wonder they had a posh uniform, with a black and red striped blazer, and winter and summer hats. So ...... when I wore this fancy dress everyone would know that I was either rich or brainy .... and no one in the Buildings was rich!

"How much do they have to pay to get in?" I asked.

"It's a lot of money – hundreds of pounds," replied Mavis – "and it's not an entrance fee 'to get in', they have to pay every term, and some of them have got two or three sisters here – all paying fees."

I could not imagine such wealth. Mum had found it very expensive to buy my uniform, and all the other things on the list, even though we had qualified for the grant. Dad wasn't unemployed anymore – there was work for everybody during the war – and he was earning much more than he used to get on the dole, but with three of us growing up, and always needing new clothes, there still never seemed to be enough to go round, and there was certainly never any left over. These girls must be really, really rich. They probably had baths with hot water, and a telephone, and a car, and they probably all went away on holidays as well!

It was Dad who had chosen this school for me. He believed it was a very good school, and now I was beginning to understand why he was so keen for me to do well in the test and why he was so pleased that I had been successful. Both Mum and Dad were very intelligent but had been denied the education and the opportunity to fulfil their potential. For Dad in particular, this seemed to be very frustrating and with failed businesses behind him and many years of unemployment he had never been an adequate breadwinner for his family. Now, his daughter was attending a posh fee-paying Grammar school, with a flashy uniform, and he could bask in the reflected glory. It restored a little of the self-respect that he had lost in those soul-destroying years.

Mum was equally pleased, but her pleasure was completely unselfish. She was relieved to think that I would have opportunities in life that had been denied to her. I could get a better job and would not have to be a servant or a cleaner as she had been. She just wanted me to be happy.

I was looking forward to life in the hostel, mixing with the upper class, and I thought I would be happy there. I went to bed that night, tucked up in the bed in the corner, underneath the hard, heavy army blankets, and for the first time in my life, with no po under the bed.

SKINNERS' COMPANY'S SCHOOL

Sunday evening came, and the girls who had gone home for the weekend were due back. I was eager to meet Billie whose bed was next to mine. She was the last to arrive, having missed the usual train, and we were already in our dormitory getting ready for lights-out. As soon as I saw her, I liked her. She had a lovely face. She was not pretty, but very elfin. Her short hair was worn in a fringe, and with her straight nose and pointed chin, she looked very prim and proper. It was not until she laughed, that you could see her sense of fun and the mischievous twinkle in her eye. She seemed pleased to meet me and I hope she had not already chosen a special friend. I was sure we would get on well together.

She lived in Cookham Buildings in Bethnal Green, in East London, and had been evacuated for the early part of the war with relatives in Derbyshire. She had three sisters and two brothers, all but one older than her, and we got on well right from the start.

Next morning was to be my first day at school.

"You'll need to take everything with you," I was advised, "because we don't come back here at lunchtime. We've got games this afternoon, so you'll need your PT kit – everything except your swimming costume."

"It's going to be quite heavy to carry it all," I said as I packed my satchel.

"That's nothing," they said, "wait until all the teachers have given you some books. We haven't got a desk so we have to lug everything around with us all day long. And there's a lot of walking to do."

"We used to have a school bus every morning," I recalled, but no such luxury here. I set off for the long walk with Billie. Skinners' School was sharing the premises on the outskirts of town with the Welwyn Garden City Grammar School. Timetables had been arranged so that the local pupils worked from 8am till 2pm, leaving the premises vacant for us during the afternoon. There was no room for us there during the morning so we had our lessons in Church Halls and Community Centres. We would start the day in the Backhouse Rooms or Friends Meeting House. The big difference from Newnham School was that we had a different teacher for every subject so they couldn't really get to know us.

As soon as the lesson ended our teacher would have to rush off to her next class, perhaps in a different part of town and we would have to wait for our next teacher. It was not unusual for a number of classes to be taught simultaneously in the same hall which could be very distracting. There were no desks, or blackboards. There were a few tables but not enough to go round, so for some lessons we sat on chairs with our books on our knees.

My first lesson was mathematics, and we were learning algebra. Although I had missed the first six weeks of term, I found it quite easy. I have never had a problem with maths, it is a very logical subject and easy to understand. French was quite a different matter. I had never heard a foreign language before and was eager to learn it, but it seemed to me that they were all speaking French fluently and I did not understand any of it. I was very impressed with the way in which they could answer Miss White's questions, and wondered when I would be able to catch up. Some of the girls in my class had come up from Lower School and they had started French in the previous year so I was a long way behind and would have a lot to learn.

Miss White was asking things in French, and then picking on someone to answer, and all of them seemed to understand. I just sat back, watching them with admiration until suddenly she picked on me.

"June," she said very slowly, "De quel couleur sont les yeux de Pierre?"

"Oh, I don't know any French," I explained, politely, thinking that it would excuse me indefinitely.

"No, I know you don't," she said, a little impatiently, "but you've got to learn. If you follow in the book, you'll see the answer! 'Ses yeux sont bleu.' His eyes are blue! Now make a little effort – it's not difficult."

I recalled my lessons with Miss Reddall, where I was always the one who knew the answer. It was going to be different from now on. All these girls were clever, and they had a good start on me and I wondered if I would ever be able to catch up.

* * * * * * * * * *

I was relieved when the morning's lessons came to an end, and we set off for lunch. My satchel, with maths and French books, was now much heavier.

Our mid-day meal was served at Trevellyan House, a community hall in the Town Centre, quite a long walk from the Backhouse Rooms. By the time we got there, there was a long queue and often the trays were very sticky. The food was not very good, although I was always hungry and ate everything.

We usually had spam fritters, corned beef or vegetable pie. The baked beans were quite nice, but the cabbage was often over-done and had lost its colour. You could always fill up on mashed potato which was made from 'Pom', dried potato powder reconstituted with water. You could tell it was not made from fresh potatoes because there were never any proper lumps in it. If you did find a lump, you could cut it in half, and it was full of dry powder.

All the puddings fell neatly into three categories – Hammer and Chisel, Stodge or Slosh. People at the back of the queue would shout, 'What's for pud?' and the reply might be 'It's hammer and chisel!' This was understood clearly to mean jam or marmalade, or some such tart, the pastry crust being so hard that when you tried to break it with your spoon, it would resist all your efforts until suddenly it would snap and shoot off your plate, either across the table or upside down into your lap.

The favoured reply to the question was 'It's stodge.' This was popular because it was filling. It was a slab of pudding, usually brown or yellow which could be detected just breaking the surface beneath a sea of custard. It always seemed, initially that there was too much custard, but the last few dry mouthfuls of stodge would have slipped down more easily with a little more lubrication.

The dreaded reply to the question was 'It's slosh!' This was the generic term for all the milk puddings served with a ladle; a dish full of semolina with a blob of jam in the middle – the challenge was to make the jam last to the final mouthful. Even worse than semolina was the disgusting tapioca. Its resemblance to frogs' spawn was unmistakeable and a better description than 'slosh' would have been 'slime'. I don't think anybody liked these sloppy liquid desserts. At Newnham School I always had a packed lunch – some sandwiches, a cake or a biscuit and an apple, but it had been suggested at the beginning of the war, that a midday meal for evacuees could be provided at a local canteen.

COMMUNAL MEALS

'......it would often be desirable to relieve householders by organising communal meals.

Where school canteens can be provided it may be possible to provide midday meals for the billeted

children at these canteens (W.V.S).'
Ministry of Health   Memo Ev 5 1939

After lunch we began the long trek to the school, on a hill on the edge of town. As we were arriving, the local Grammar School pupils were leaving, having finished for the day after their early start.

Our form mistress was Miss White, our French teacher, and I had not made a very good first impression on her. The Registers were kept at the school to save carrying them to the Halls every morning, so we had to answer our names for morning and afternoon sessions. We would respond "Early, early, please." or perhaps, "Late, early, please" if we had not got to school on time, or "Late excused, early, please," if, for example, we had had a morning dental appointment.

She would read out any important notices, but that was about all we saw of our Form Mistress. She would not get to know us like Miss Reddall.

The facilities at the school were good: there were netball courts and hockey pitches; there was a gymnasium with wall bars, vaulting equipment and climbing ropes; and there were specialist subject rooms for needlework and cookery, and well-equipped science laboratories.

I remember with some amusement my first year's needlework lessons with Miss Pickard. Our first project was to make an apron with large front pockets in which our work could be kept. We embroidered our names in chain stitch. Then we could move on to proper dressmaking. Our summer uniform was a gingham dress, in a choice of red, blue or green. In preparation

162

for the summer we were to make a pair of matching knickers. Now, gingham material does not stretch, so the style was balloon-like to allow for movement. We had to choose one of the colours and I chose my favourite colour which was green. Week after week, I was cutting, tacking and trying to get the gussets in the right place, and not making very much progress. Some girls, whose parents lived in the area, were able to get help at home and were well ahead of me. Kitty King came into class one day. Her mother had bought her a green dress and she asked if anyone with green knickers would like to swap for a pair of nearly finished blue ones. I looked at my pile of bits of materials pinned together incorrectly and said that I didn't mind changing, but I still had not finished tacking. She was delighted, and relieved me of all my bits and pieces in exchange for a pair of billowing blue bloomers which required only the elastic. By the following lesson, Kitty had finished her green knickers and we were both happy – but I don't ever remember wearing them!

We were lucky to have the facilities at the Grammar School – sewing machines, sports equipment, science labs, and so on. It would have been nice to have had them all day and to have had our own desks where we could have left our books, and lockers for our equipment, instead of lugging them around town all day, but when there's a war on you can't have everything. I think most evacuees had their education disrupted in one way or another. Some never spent more than a year in one school before being moved on, and after the war, my brother John said he had never once, during five years of secondary education, had a science lesson in a laboratory. I could not imagine how you can learn science without access to Bunsen burners and test tubes and all the other scientific equipment found only in a lab.

At the end of our school day, we had the long walk back to the hostel, our satchels now even heavier. The straps cut into our shoulders, and we frequently transferred the weight from one side to the other.

HOSTEL DUTIES

I enjoyed hostel life, it was good to be with your friends. Before dinner we had an hour and a half for 'prep'. This was our homework, and it was ages before I realised that it was short for 'preparation' for the next lesson. We worked at the tables in the Dining Room and had to be finished by the time they wanted to lay them for our evening meal. Food in the hostel was better than in Trevellyan House, but it was still wartime food. We rarely had meat, but had plenty of vegetables. Potatoes and baked beans were served regularly, and it was in the hostel that I first tasted dried egg. This, like 'Pom', required only the addition of water, or a little milk and could then be used for omelettes, scrambled eggs or in cake-making. Obviously it was no substitute for a fried or poached egg, but the production of eggs was very labour intensive and on the whole, fresh eggs were only regularly available to people like Uncle 'erbert, who were able to keep their own chickens.

Scrambled eggs or omelettes made with dried egg powder were an acquired taste. Even seasoned with salt and pepper, it did not taste like fresh eggs, but with regular use it became familiar and quite acceptable. I remember after the war when the real thing became available again, finding it quite difficult to get used to the original taste.

Unlike Trevellyan House, we had plenty of fresh potatoes but the quantity depended upon the amount that had been peeled the night before.

'Peeling Potatoes' was one of the duties which was assigned to us on the rota. A duty list was posted on the notice board every week. The worst duty, in my opinion, was 'Washing Up'. This was in the days before detergents had been discovered and the water was always greasy. We had to put a few handfuls of soda into the water, which softened it but did not dissolve the grease. I hated searching for a few teaspoons at the bottom of a big bowl, with nasty bits of cabbage clinging to your fingers like seaweed. We were not encouraged to change the water as hot water used precious fuel.

A team of girls would be responsible for 'Drying Up', and in their rush to finish, they seldom gave the plates time to drain which meant that the tea-cloths were soon soggy and too wet to be effective.

The duty I liked best was 'Potatoes'. There had been one occasion when there were hardly enough to go round. Billie and I would have liked some more, but they were all gone.

"Who was on 'Potatoes' last night?" we complained, "You didn't do enough!"

The following week when it was our turn, we decided to peel loads of them every night. We did not mind how long it took us, because we could talk while we were working, and we knew we would be able to have second helpings for dinner next day. It was wonderful because, as well as seconds, we had them fried up for breakfast. Not surprisingly, we were given this duty together quite often.

One of the duties which could not be allocated to the younger girls was 'Blackout and Coals'. The coal scuttles were too heavy for them to lift and the blackout time was quite late in the summer. 'Blackout' was very important. Every window had to be covered before lighting-up time so that not even the smallest chink of light could be seen from the outside. All the windows had thick heavy curtains, usually black, grey or dark green with a generous overlap. Street wardens would parade through the town to check that they had been properly drawn and if they were not satisfied they would knock heavily on the door, shouting 'Lights!' This was a kind reminder because failing to cover the windows properly could result in a fine.

The other part of this duty was 'Coals', which applied only during the winter.Coal-scuttles had to be filled and fires stoked as and when necessary. The irritating part of this duty was when you were sitting comfortably in an armchair by a coal fire, someone from another room would shout 'Coal' and you had to go and see to it. By the time you got back you had lost your armchair.

Nobody ever complained about having to do duties. It seemed to be a sensible way of sharing the work. We were growing up and had to accept our share of the responsibility for day to day living.

With homework to do, and duties every day, there seemed very little time for leisure, but on the whole, life in the hostel was very enjoyable. I liked being with my friends, twenty-four hours a day, and many close relationships were formed, many of which have stood the test of time.

CHICKEN-POX

As the end of the Autumn term approached, two events seemed to be predictable – assuming that you were not bombed out of existence. The first was the end of term exams and the second was going home for Christmas, my first Christmas at home for 5 years. How wrong can you be!

I was dreading the exams and knew I would do badly. We had been given a list of topics to revise for each subject, and a few hints about the exam questions. Some of the questions related to work which had been completed before I started. You cannot revise work that you have not already done.

I suppose the teachers would have made allowances, but I didn't want the humiliation of coming bottom. The exams were timetabled to begin on Monday 13th December (which was Billie's birthday). They would take place in the afternoons in the main school building where we had desks to sit at. There seemed to be no way out, but no one could have predicted a chicken-pox epidemic. Some of the girls, including Billie, had gone home for the previous weekend and had not returned, having had the infection confirmed. Lucky them! They would miss the exams and have a long Christmas holiday. How I envied them. How could I catch it? All I wanted was a few spots. I kept examining my skin, looking for the first signs of a rash. I was not disappointed. On Monday morning I noticed a few small spots.

"Look, I've got some spots on my arm. I've got a rash. I think I've got chicken-pox." I felt a rush of excitement as I went round showing everyone. "I'm going to the medical room."

I sat in the waiting room, not really thinking that I had chicken-pox, hoping that my spots would not disappear before I had been examined.

"I've got this rash," I explained, "and I feel very itchy."

"Take off your jumper and your blouse," said the nurse, and she examined my back.

"It's on my arms," I told her. "Yes," she agreed, "and on your back as well. Yes, it is chicken-pox. Get dressed and wait outside."

I would have to go back to the hostel and pack my case. I thought there was a train at about 2 o'clock, but that would be a bit of a rush if I was going to have my dinner first. It would be better to have my dinner at Trevellyan House, then go back to the hostel to pack and catch the later train. I had it all worked out.

I sat there, contemplating my good fortune at missing the exams and congratulating myself on this perfect timing. The nurse came out of the medical room.

"May I go now, please?" I asked, "I'd like to buy my train ticket before I go to Trevellyan House for dinner."

"I'm sorry, June, you won't be able to go to Trevellyan House. You are not allowed to mix with any of the other pupils. Chicken-pox is very contagious. And you won't to be allowed to go on a train, either, or any other public transport."

"Well, how am I going to get home?" I asked.

"I'm sorry, June," she replied, "you're not going to be able to go home. You're going to have to go into hospital. We are waiting for the ambulance."

"Hospital? What hospital?"

"You are going to the Isolation Hospital in St Albans."

"How long for?" I asked in disbelief.

"I'm afraid you'll have to stay there until you are declared free from chicken-pox, and that will be three weeks!"

"Three weeks? But I'll miss Christmas," I said, "I can't go in for three weeks!"

"Well, I'm afraid there's no alternative," and I started to cry.

168

THE ISOLATION HOSPITAL

I had never been in an ambulance before. If I had been carried in, on a stretcher with a broken leg perhaps, I probably would have felt quite important, especially if I had been surrounded by sympathisers and well-wishers. I just felt wretched. By the time the ambulance arrived, everyone had gone to lunch and were probably laughing and joking as usual about slosh, stodge and hammer and chisel. There was no one left to say goodbye or wish me luck. I climbed into the back of the ambulance and they shut the doors, and I started to cry again.

I had never been in a hospital before, but even if I had it would not have prepared me for St Albans Isolation Hospital. I thought it was the hospital which would be isolated – perhaps on a hill outside the town, where no one could catch our germs, which would be blown away in the wind. Naively I had not realised that it was the patients who were isolated – even from each other. There were no wards or communal facilities, no public areas, and of course, no visitors – just glass rooms.

In my block there were four of these cells in a row and I was put in the first one. It was like being in a fish tank. The next two were empty but I could see another prisoner in the end cubicle. I now knew the meaning of the word 'isolation'. No one to play with or even to talk to. For three weeks! Every time I thought of the words 'three weeks', I burst into tears.

The nurse came in carrying a blue hospital gown. "Take off all your clothes and put this gown on."

"It looks too big," I replied sulkily.

"Well, it will be all right for now," she assured me. "I'll see if I can find a smaller one tomorrow. When you've got it on, the doctor will be coming in to see you."

169

"Can I go to the toilet first?" I asked, trying to think of an excuse to get out of this fish tank.

"There's your toilet," she said, pointing to the piece of furniture between the two beds. "It's a commode." She lifted up the hinged lid to reveal a white bedpan. This was like being back with a po under the bed, but it would be even worse because other people would be able to see what you'd done. I started to cry again.

"Don't cry," she said, putting her arms round me, "you can pull the curtain round when you need to use it, and I'll bring you some books to read. I'll be back in about five minutes," and with that she left, locking the door from the outside.

This was worse than being in prison. At least prisoners were allowed out of their cells for a little while each day for exercise or to go to the workshops, and of course, they were allowed to sit together at meal times. And if the prisoners didn't like being locked up in a cell – well, it was their own fault because they had broken the law. I had done nothing wrong and I was to be locked up for three weeks. And I burst into tears again. I thought of the lepers in the Bible stories, who were not allowed to mix with other people, and they had to ring a bell as they walked around shouting 'Unclean! Unclean!'

And of course, this was a hospital for people suffering from highly contagious diseases, so outsiders were not allowed in. There were no visiting hours. Nobody was allowed to come and sit by your bed, bringing sweets and chocolates and eating your grapes. This was complete isolation and it was for three weeks. I would miss Christmas, and the whole of the Christmas holiday, which I had been looking forward to so much. It was to have been my first Christmas at home since 1938, the first for five years! I couldn't stop crying. This was cruel. It seemed then, as it does now, the unhappiest time of the war, and probably the most miserable time in my life.

I wanted so much to spend Christmas at home and instead I was locked up here as a prisoner. For a while my thoughts turned to making an escape. I didn't know how far St Albans was from London, but the farthest it could be was the twenty miles from Welwyn Garden City to London plus the distance of the ambulance journey. We might even be nearer to London than Welwyn Garden City.

I had some money – enough for my train fare home - but I didn't know where the station was and I knew I was not allowed to travel on public transport anyway. I could spread chicken-pox through the whole country if there were other people on the train. I thought of walking – I could even run some of the way – but I wouldn't know which way to go. There were no signposts. I remembered that they had all been taken down at the beginning of the war because of the possibility of enemy spies being dropped into the countryside by parachute, and we didn't want them to know exactly where they were. They might be trying to get to London or to important places which they wanted to destroy; to railway junctions where they could disrupt transport; to factories where ammunitions were being made or aeroplanes being built. They might even want to destroy our hospitals. This had all been explained to us in 1940, when the signposts had been taken down and the names of the towns removed.

As well as refusing to give directions to strangers we had to be very careful not to say anything which would help the enemy.

Government posters and broadcasts warned us of the dangers of giving away our secrets, explaining that lives could be at risk 'Careless Talk Costs Lives'.

Now the boot was on the other foot, and I knew that no one would help me on my way. If I went in daylight hours, I would soon be spotted in my blue hospital gown as they had taken all my clothes away to be fumigated. If I went after dark, I knew I would get lost. All the towns were in complete darkness during the blackout and it was very dangerous. All the buildings had heavy blackout curtains at every window and there were no street lights. During the first three months of the blackout, the number of fatal accidents on the roads was more than doubled. It would be very frightening.

Escaping was just a silly idea which I realised would not work, and I burst into tears again. Three weeks! It seemed like a life sentence. Chicken-pox was just a common childhood infection, and to isolate us like this seemed to be going to drastic and unnecessary lengths. However, the school had no choice, as they were following a government directive, issued at the beginning of the war to prevent the spread of infectious diseases.

INFECTIOUS DISEASES

It is important that provision should be made against the increased risk of the epidemic spread of infectious disease, and the local authority should make adequate provision for the isolation and treatment of cases of infectious disease.

Ministry of Health   Memo Ev 5 1939

Two miserable days passed. The tears subsided but the misery remained. The books they had given me were boring and I spent much of the time watching white robed doctors and nurses walking past my glass box, often wearing masks over their faces.

I thought of my friends at school, doing their exams, and envied them. I would rather have been doing the exams, even if I came bottom, than be stuck in this lonely boring glass fish-tank.

The nurse came in looking cheerful. "I've got some good news for you!" she said.

"Am I going home?" I asked hopefully.

"No, I'm sorry, you can't go home, but you are going to have a friend to keep you company. Another pupil from Skinners has been admitted, and she's in reception now. She can share this ward with you."

"What's her name?" I asked, hoping it would be someone I liked.

"Nesta Majeron," replied the nurse, "Do you know her?"

My heart sank. Nesta Majeron was not in my year. "I think she's in the Fourth Form," I replied, expecting a sympathetic response from the nurse. "Or even the Upper Fourth," I added. "She'll be 13, or even 14, and I'm only 11!"

The horror of this seemed to be completely lost on the nurse. How could you spend three weeks with someone so old. We never played with girls in the class above, but because we went to the same school, and both had chicken-pox, the nurses assumed we would be friends!

Then I thought of another problem. Nesta was Jewish. I had never met any Jewish people until I came to Skinners, and in my first two months at the school, which had more Jews than

Christians, it didn't seem to make any difference. But this was Christmas, and the Jews believe in the Old Testament, but not the New Testament, and we believe in the New Testament as well.

Everything about Christmas was in the New Testament. I didn't know if they sent Christmas cards and had presents, and whether they decorated trees with tinsel and lights. Perhaps Nesta would not mind being in hospital as much as I did. I would have to be careful what I said to her, and I could certainly not say anything about The Baby Jesus.

Nesta arrived and smiled shyly when she saw me. I smiled back, and an uneasy silence followed.

"That's your bed," I said, trying to think of something to say to break the ice, although I realised it was a silly thing to have said because she could see that my bed had been slept in.

The nurse gave Nesta a hospital gown to put on and left us alone. Neither of us could think of anything to talk about.

"We can't go outside to the toilet, we have to use that," I explained, pointing to the commode.

"Oh," was all she said in reply. That was going to be a big embarrassment, because even if we used the curtain, we would be able to hear what the other one was doing – oh, and even worse – we would be able to smell it!

I was beginning to think that the next nineteen days, sharing a cell with Nesta, was going to be even worse than being alone.

I soon realised that I needed to go on the commode. I was wishing that I hadn't had two glasses of lemonade, and regretted that I hadn't used the commode before Nesta had arrived.

The minutes dragged by, and I couldn't pluck up my

174

courage to say I wanted to wee. It was going to be so humiliating. I was so wrapped up in my own misery that I was quite unaware of Nesta's feelings. Suddenly I realised that it was just as bad for her. I don't know what had brought about the change – I think perhaps she must have glanced at the commode – but I knew that she wanted to go as well. It was just the same for her. We were in the same boat. It was probably worse for her because she was older, and because she hadn't used it before.

I looked at her and said, "Who's going to go first?" and we both burst out laughing. It was a relief of tension. "You go first," said Nesta, "and then I'll go."

We both used the commode, and then drew back the curtain. It was a very levelling experience. We realised we were in the same boat. Neither of us wanted to be here, and we didn't want to be with each other. But we had no choice, and we had to make the best of it. We might as well be friends and try to enjoy it. We were going to spend Christmas together, and the New Year.

We made up games to play. We were good mimics 'Guess who this is?' we would say, and one by one, our teachers were brought to life by our uninhibited impersonations. Then 'Who walks like this?' and again they were all identified as we stomped or shuffled round the room, accompanied by shrieks of laughter.

Our beds became trampolines and our pillows were missiles.

Christmas was approaching and the nurses had brought us some packets of coloured paper strips for making paper chains. We glued the links together and decorated our cell. It looked very festive, with sprigs of holly and other greenery. I need not have worried about Nesta being Jewish. She enjoyed making the paper chains and seemed to be looking forward to the celebrations.

On Christmas Day, the nurses wore paper hats and served our dinner in style. We listened to the wireless and sang Christmas Carols. It was not like Christmas at home, but we made the best of it, and enjoyed ourselves.

The remaining days passed, and the blisters dried up and turned to scabs – in spite of the warnings about being scarred for life if you picked them, it was impossible to leave them alone. They bled when you scratched them, and another scab formed, until finally you were declared spotless and free from infection.

Mum came to collect me and I said goodbye to Nesta. We had had some fun together. Fourteen-year-olds are not so bad when you get to know them.

I had only three days at home, before it was time to return to Welwyn Garden City for the Spring term but all my presents were waiting for me, and Mum cooked us another Christmas dinner especially for me. It was far from being my happiest Christmas but it is still probably the most memorable.

AIR-RAIDS AND SHELTERS

Life in Welwyn Garden City was quite different from being in Radwell. No one really looked after me any more. When I was with Auntie Edie and Uncle 'erbert it was like being with your family. Auntie Edie was quite old, and never seemed to worry about whether I had cleaned my teeth or not, but it was still like being in the family.

In Welwyn Garden City, none of the grown-ups really knew me, and as long as I did not break any rules, everything was all right.

Gone were the carefree days of catching grasshoppers and making daisy chains. Now it was a question of making my own bed, doing homework, checking the rota for duties and not talking after 'lights-out'. No one would be asking me to stand on the chair to sing carols any more.

I accepted all this, and enjoyed life in the hostel and although I was not fully aware of it at the time, I can see now that as my life had changed, so too, I had to change. I grew up. I was now old enough to buy a half-price ticket to London and go home for the weekend. I think we were allowed to go about once a month and I always went with Billie. She was now becoming a very close friend, and we were always together. We shared a common interest in sport and we were both in the under-13 years netball team, and loved our gym lessons.

She lived in Cookham Buildings in Bethnal Green, which was not much better than Peabody, and her home background was similar to mine. We would travel to King's Cross together, and meet again on Sunday evening for the journey back.

I remember with pride, as we passed through North London on the train, drawing her attention to a big advertisement painted on the wall of a public house which said,

'THE BUILDERS ARMS – SIMPSONS BALDOCK ALES'

"That's where Uncle 'erbert works. He makes that beer," I boasted, "I know, I've been to the brewery." I'm sure Billie was very impressed.

When we reached King's Cross, we went our separate ways, Billie on the Northern Line to Old Street, while I walked to Herbrand Street. Nobody ever met me at the station, I was quite capable of managing on my own.

I turned the corner of Tavistock Place into Herbrand Street and had quite a shock. It looked different. The railings had gone, and the big iron gates. The low wall was still there, about eighteen inches high, but that was all that separated G and H blocks from the pavement.

It looked very bare. "What's happened to the railings?" I asked, as soon as I got in.

"They've taken all the iron to make aeroplanes," was the explanation.

"I bet the people in G block and H Block don't like it much, especially at night with people walking up the street."

"Well, they didn't have any choice and they've taken the railings from nearly everywhere."

"Will they put them back after the war?" I asked.

"I don't know," said Mum, "we'll have to wait and see."

"And have they taken them down from outside Buckingham Palace as well?" I asked, thinking of the magnificent black iron gates and railings topped with gold, which we could peer through as we watched the ceremonial 'Changing of The Guard'. Mum did not know, but even as I asked we both knew instinctively that they would still be safely in place.

I soon got used to seeing the Buildings without the railings even though it still looked rather bare, but if the iron could be used to make aeroplanes which would help to win the war, then I agreed it was a good idea.

It was not only our buildings which looked bare. When I went to the corner of the street at the junction with Coram Street, it wasn't just iron railings which were missing. The houses had gone. They used to back on to F Block where Grandma lived in no. 14. When a bomb was very close, the windows would rattle and sometimes the ornaments on the mantelpiece would fall off. Grandma must have been very frightened.

In Radwell I had lived the war through the wireless. Now I was living it for real. I saw the bombing and the devastation and I experienced the uneasy apprehension of wondering what the next air-raid would bring.

The warning siren wailed continuously – up and down, up and down, and it was the most melancholy sound I had ever heard.

Some people ran straight to the shelters. Others could be seen hurrying home with their shopping. Mothers waited anxiously for children to come running home, although it wouldn't really make much difference, as they would not be able to protect their children if the bomb fell on them. I think they must have felt as I had, that it was important for families to be together. We all wanted to live, but not without the rest of our family.

The shelters were cramped and very claustrophobic and not everyone used them. Some preferred to trust to luck. It was like a lottery and if your number came up .... Well of course, some were unlucky and lost their homes or their lives.

We huddled in the shelter, nothing to do except hope and pray that we would not be the unlucky ones today. Some people waited silently, and others joked facetiously to keep up our spirits, and to conceal their deep anxiety.

A cheer went up when the 'all-clear' sounded. It was the same siren, but now on a continuous high uninterrupted note. The relief that was felt was almost tangible.

Some boys ran into the yard shouting, "They've got Leigh Street, there are three in Leigh Street," and they ran off in that direction. I hoped it was not the Fish and Chip shop. Leigh Street was only a few blocks away, between home and King's Cross. The word went round. "It's Leigh Street," and we followed in hot pursuit as though it would have disappeared if we had not been quick. I don't know whether our excitement to see the damage was a gesture of relief that it was not us who had been hit, or whether it was just a ghoulish morbid interest which motivated us. We ran all the way and then stared in horror at the pile of smoking rubble where there had been familiar houses. There was a strong acrid smell which I shall never forget.

The rescue services were stretched to full capacity as they were called to many sites simultaneously. They did not have the time or the manpower to cordon off the area and we could stand as close as we liked as long as we did not get in their way.

"There are a lot of people in there," they were saying, "Some may still be alive."

You could not imagine anyone living under that rubble with that acrid smell and the smoke, but miracles do happen. It would take hours, or even days, to clear the site and eventually we went home, very subdued, having seen what war was all about. Most of us had collected pieces of shrapnel, the remains of the exploded bomb, to take home as souvenirs. The larger pieces were the most highly valued, but we did not need anything to remind us of what we had seen – we would never forget it

* * * * * * * * *

The London Underground became a favourite refuge for people to stay overnight, especially in those stations which were very deep. At first, people were discouraged from using them as they were potentially dangerous, but it was soon accepted that the people would not go away and they had to be accommodated. The electricity on the lines was turned off for safety reasons after the last train had gone through and people set up camp on the platforms and in the connecting corridors. People arrived with camp beds, sleeping bags and primus stoves and set up base for the night. They had concerts underground to raise morale, and a strong feeling of camaraderie developed amongst the campers.

The safety record of underground stations was excellent as far as bomb damage was concerned, but they were not without their disasters. Bethnal Green station was used regularly as a shelter and could accommodate ten thousand people in bunk beds, and a further five thousand in the connecting corridors. When an air-raid warning sounded, people who were near a station would run for cover. In 1943, a tragedy occurred, the cause of which is not clear. Very loud explosions were heard in the East End of London and people, assuming that it was enemy aircraft, ran for cover. There was, however, no air-raid at the time and probably no enemy aircraft overhead. It is thought likely that the explosions were caused by a military exercise testing new anti-aircraft guns in the nearby Victoria Park. Whatever the reason, people panicked and rushed to get into Bethnal Green Underground air-raid shelter. It is believed that someone at the bottom of a flight of stairs tripped over and the surging mass behind caused a pile-up in which nearly 200 people were crushed to death. A plaque to commemorate the tragedy can still be seen at the station.

IN MEMORY OF THE 173 MEN, WOMEN AND CHILDREN WHO LOST THEIR LIVES ON THE EVENING OF 3RD MARCH 1943 DESCENDING THESE STEPS TO BETHNAL GREEN UNDERGROUND AIR RAID SHELTER.
NOT FORGOTTEN."

CHISLEHURST CAVES

Another obvious choice for safety from the bombing were the Chislehurst Caves in Kent. At first, it was on a casual basis, with local people sheltering in the entrance, bringing with them deck chairs, camp beds and torches. The caves were situated conveniently on a commuter line from Charing Cross and Cannon Street, and during the blitz of 1940, people began to arrive from farther afield in special 'Caves Trains'.

Chislehurst Caves

The caves, which were man-made, date back hundreds of years, and were in fact mines yielding a valuable source of chalk and flint. The tunnels, covering an area of three and a half acres, eventually provided shelter for fifteen thousand people, and as the numbers increased, amenities improved. Electricity was laid on, and crude sanitation installed. The caves were divided into sections, ventilation shafts bored, and strict discipline was monitored by the 'Cave Captains', each being responsible for a designated area. A charge was made of one penny per night or sixpence per week.

CAVE RULES

1. No admission or re-entry to the Dormitory Section after 9.30 p.m. (10 p.m. Double Summer Time).

2. Shelterers already asleep in the Main Caves must not be disturbed by people coming to their pitches.

3. Pitches must be kept clean.

4. No furniture admitted.

5. Stoves of all kinds prohibited.

6. Rubbish must be placed in the Bins.

7. Children should be in their pitches by 9 p.m. and stay there.

8. Unauthorised sale of goods is prohibited.

9. There must be reasonable quiet by 10 p.m.

10. Lights out and absolute silence by 10.30 p.m. in the Dormitory Section.

11. Pitches must not be changed, exchanged or sold.

12. Four Days absence may involve loss of pitch.

13. The Cave Captain controls his section.

14. Music must cease by 9 p.m.

15. Organised concerts can only be held by permission.

16. Breach of Rules involves loss of pitch.

17. Arrive early and stay put.

It became an underground city; the Red Cross opened a fully staffed medical centre; the W.V.S. provided a canteen; a church was consecrated with its own choir, and there was a smaller chapel for the children; there were evening classes and entertainment, a gymnasium for keep-fit, a hairdressers and a library; and the caves had their own Scouts, Guides and Brownies packs.

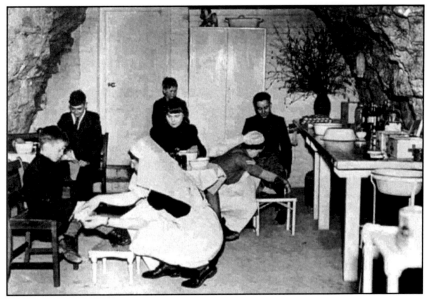

'The Red Cross Hospital' 1942

The number of people seeking refuge in the caves fluctuated with the intensity of the bombing, and at busy times it was sometimes necessary to post notices at Charing Cross Station, saying 'Caves Full'.

The numbers of the individual pitches were painted on the walls and can still be seen today, giving some idea how the 'city' operated.

The Germans were aware of the existence of the caves and of their use as an air-raid shelter. They were referred to by 'Lord Haw Haw' in his radio broadcasts. William Joyce was a renegade Englishman and a Nazi propagandist who travelled to Germany at the outbreak of the war to offer his services to the enemy.

He used the name 'Lord Haw Haw' throughout the war and his broadcasts from Hamburg could be picked up regularly on the wireless. He spoke with a very upper middle-class accent, and always began by saying, 'Germany Calling, Germany Calling'. He said that the rats in Chislehurst Caves would be ferreted out and exterminated.

Joyce was arrested in Flensburg after the war, charged with 'High Treason', and was eventually hanged in 1946, aged 40, as a traitor.

Air-raid shelters were an important feature in the lives of many people – especially in the big cities. Winston Churchill needed somewhere safe and secure to work with his War Cabinet. Such was the importance of his role in the war that evacuation was considered, and many different sites were explored. Eventually it was decided to find a shelter near to the home of government, and a building near Whitehall was found, not far from his home in Downing Street.

The 'Office of Works' building, facing St James' Park in Horseguards Road proved to be an ideal location. Churchill, his War Cabinet, his Intelligence Organisation and his staff, met below ground in the fortified basement known as 'The Cabinet War Rooms', which offered shelter from air-raids, and a place to work, sleep and live for as long as necessary.

The entrance to what is now a museum, can still be seen today, heavily sandbagged, for added safety.

The Cabinet War Rooms

Not many shelters were as sophisticated as The Cabinet War Rooms. The simplest and most basic were the corrugated steel Anderson shelters which were dug into the ground and covered by earth. They provided temporary shelter for the duration of an air-raid. Although they were very simple, they were known to have saved lives in areas of heavy bombing.

An Anderson shelter

On my weekend visits to London I sought refuge in our shelter in the yard whenever there was an air-raid.

I would usually catch the 6.40 train on Sunday evening to be back in the hostel in time for 'lights-out'. On one occasion, just before I was due to leave home, the warning siren sounded and we ran to the shelter. By the time the raid was over, it was too late for me to travel back that evening. It was agreed that I should stay in London overnight and catch the early train to be in time for school. It was during a period of heavy night bombing, and we decided to sleep in the shelter. John was in Hitchin and Dad always slept in the flat, so Mum, Basil and I gathered together the things we needed and went down to the shelter. Facilities there were very basic. The brick walls had been painted white, and it was packed quite closely with two-tier and three-tier bunks. Mum had the bottom bunk and Basil was above me.

The facilities were minimal; there was a kettle and a teapot on a small table with a primus stove and a few cups. There was a washbasin with a jug of cold water and a bar of soap. A chemical toilet was situated in the corner of the room, separated from the sleeping area by a thin partition. You could hear what everyone was doing in there. The walls were covered with graffiti and someone had written '*A penny on the drum – sweet music*'.

I climbed into my bunk, hoping that I would not oversleep, as I dare not miss the early morning train. This was obviously on my mind as I went to sleep. The next thing I remember was hearing a woman saying, "Take her back to her bunk, she's still asleep."

When she said that, I was awake. I realised I'd been sleepwalking and I felt very embarrassed. I was over by the door, on my way to the station. The easiest thing to do was to pretend I was still asleep and let her lead me back to my bunk. I went back quietly, and no one mentioned it in the morning, but I wondered how far I would have got on my journey back to Welwyn Garden City if I had not been stopped by friendly neighbours.

While we were sheltering from enemy bombing, our Air Force was regularly bombing Germany. Civilian lives were being lost on both sides. The brave pilots and crew of these heavy planes were always risking their lives and many were brought down, not to return home. Those who returned safely, to fight another day, were welcomed as heroes and a popular wartime song pays tribute to their courage and bravery.

Over the dim lit flare path

An anxious silence reigned

Scanning the blue horizon

Our anxious eyes were strained

The radio sets were humming

They waited for a word

Then a voice broke through the humming

And this is what we heard

Coming in on a wing and a prayer

Coming in on a wing and a prayer

Though there's one motor gone

We can still carry on

Coming in on a wing and a prayer

What a show, what a fight
Yes we really hit our target for tonight

How we sing as we limp through the air
Look below, there's our field over there
With a full crew aboard
And our trust in the Lord
We're coming in on a wing and a prayer

* * * * * * * * * *

Back in the hostel at Valley Road, the Spring Term passed uneventfully. Nesta and I smiled at each other when we passed, but we were both glad to be back with our peer groups.

A NEW BILLET

Hostel life suited me. I was gregarious, and enjoyed community life, but sadly, it was not to last. Whenever billets in the town with local families became available, we were moved out. Ideally, they wanted all the hostel places to be vacant by the summer, in order to accommodate the new intake of eleven-year-olds. Mrs Walker, the warden, called me into her office. I knew what to expect, because other girls had already been moved.

"June," she said, "we've found a billet for you and you can move out on Saturday."

"Where am I going?"

"You're going to Mrs Cuss, at 19 Valley Road."

'19 Valley Road! That's next door,' I thought. Mrs Walker

knew what I was thinking. I would be able to see my friends every evening, and I wouldn't have far to go when I left them. I would be able to do my homework with them and I wouldn't have to do any duties!

"When you have moved," she continued, "you will not be allowed to come back into the hostel."

That was a big disappointment, but at least I would be able to walk to and from school with my friends until they too were billeted out, so I was not too unhappy about moving. I wondered whether it would be like living with Auntie Edie and Uncle 'erbert.

It was not! Mrs Cuss was much younger than Auntie Edie. She was quite big, and very well dressed with an immaculate hairdo. She spoke in a very posh voice, and was the forerunner of 'Hyacinth Bucket' (pronounced Bouquet) in 'Keeping Up Appearances'. I could not imagine her kissing me goodnight.

Like Hyacinth Bucket, she had the house to match. Everything was perfect. There were expensive looking ornaments and crystal glass on the polished sideboard, and two large silver candlesticks. Pride of place was given to a photograph of her daughter Muriel, which was in an ornate silver frame. A magnificent clock chimed every hour and there were large armchairs which you could tell were comfortable even before you sat down on them. They were the sort of chairs where you would have to sit still.

Mr Cuss was a banker who commuted to London every day with his leather briefcase.

Mrs Cuss took me upstairs to my room. I was to sleep in Muriel's bedroom while she was away at college. What luxury! Rose-patterned wallpaper; matching curtains which could be closed by pulling a cord; thick soft fitted carpet, a satin eiderdown and lace runners on the dressing table – and it was all very pink and fit for a princess.

"You must always do your homework downstairs," said Mrs Cuss. "Please do not bring your pen or any ink into the bedroom. You can leave your satchel downstairs," and I readily agreed.

The bed was soft and warm and comfortable, so different from the army camp beds with their hard grey blankets. I thought I was very lucky to be living in such splendour and luxury, even though it was a bit intimidating.

I returned from school one evening to be confronted by a very angry Mrs Cuss. "I thought I told you that you were not to take your pen or ink into the bedroom."

"But I didn't," I protested, "I always do my homework downstairs. I've never taken my pen or ink upstairs."

"Don't lie," she said, taking me up to the bedroom. "What's that, then?" she asked, pointing to the large blue stain on the dressing table runner. It certainly did look like ink but I couldn't explain it.

"I don't know how it got there, but I know I didn't bring my pen or ink upstairs."

"Well, they wouldn't have come up on their own, so you must have brought them up."

It was a mystery. I protested my innocence but clearly Mrs Cuss did not believe me.

A few weeks later it happened again. Two more blue stains appeared on the white lace runner. But this time the mystery was solved.

One of our school rules, strictly observed, was that shoulder-length hair had to be tied back. My hair was now long enough to be worn in plaits, secured with navy blue ribbons and elastic bands. I liked my bows to be wide and open, but gradually they got screwed up and look untidy. I would wash them under the tap and wind them round my fingers to flatten them, and then leave them pressed down on a flat surface to dry. By the following morning, they were dry and looked as though they had been ironed. It had not occurred to me that the dye would run, and I was shocked when I picked them up and saw more blue stains.

I explained to Mrs Cuss what had happened, and apologised. It was a silly thing to do, but I didn't know that the colour could come out. My honour was restored, but she did not say that she was sorry that she had not believed me, and had accused me of lying. I felt vindicated, albeit thoughtless, but I knew I had spoilt the beautiful bedroom.

* * * * * * * * *

The Easter holidays came to an end, and it was back to school for the Summer Term. One of the first things we had to do in class was to choose our Form Prefect and Games Captain. Three or four girls would be nominated and seconded for each office, and then the class would vote. The Form Prefect was usually somebody clever and well-behaved. I never actually discovered what they had to do, apart from wearing the 'Prefect's' Badge, as I was never nominated for that exalted position.

Rosemary Sands nominated me for Games Captain. I couldn't believe it. She was one of the girls who was both clever and sporty – good at everything. She was highly respected and influential. I was seconded and, having shown my ability in the gym and on the netball court, I was voted in. I would love Rosemary for the rest of my life. I was always a little in awe of her. She was very pretty, with a round face and turned up nose and beautiful black hair. You could tell she came from a very good Jewish family, and spoke with an upper-class accent. I would have loved to have been like her. She was extremely clever, hardworking and well-behaved, but with an enormous sense of fun.

Now, thanks to her, I was Games Captain. What an honour! We did not play netball in the summer term, but we would have gym and rounders and when the open-air pool opened on May 1st, we would be having swimming lessons as well.

Miss Rapp, the PT Teacher, explained my duties and responsibilities, all of which I took very seriously: get the posts out for rounders; count the bats and balls as they went out and check them all back in at the end of the lesson, and most important of all, prepare the team lists for games lessons and pin them on the wall in the classroom in advance. I was besieged by requests but I had to be fair.

"Can I try bowling, please?" I would be asked.

"Well, I've put you down at 1st Post today, because you are good at catching. You may be able to bowl next week."

"Don't put me as a deep fielder, because I can't throw in to 4th Post."

"Well, throw to 2nd Post, and they can pass it on."

All this responsibility and power! I loved it. I was conscientious and fair and I grew in confidence. It didn't seem to matter quite so much that I was struggling in French, and that I still got confused with verbs and nouns. Sport was my forté and I was going to be a good Captain.

May 1ˢᵗ arrived, and the swimming pool opened for the summer. I was really excited. There had been no pool in Baldock, so this was to be my first attempt at swimming. I was quite sure that I would be successful.

The pool was on the side of a hill on the outskirts of town. Although the sun was shining, there was a cool breeze blowing. We emerged from the wooden cubicles, wearing our navy blue woollen regulation costumes and with our towels round our shoulders. I tucked my hair inside my rubber hat and fastened the strap under my chin.

Miss Rapp blew her whistle. "Please listen carefully," she said, "Those who can swim in deep water and jump in, please stand over there by the deep end."

A group of girls moved towards the end of the pool and lined up. I was surprised to see June Rogers amongst this group of girls. June was tall and thin and not at all a sporty type. She wasn't much good at netball or rounders, and didn't excel at anything in the gym. I would have expected her to be one of the non-swimmers.

"Those who can swim in shallow water, please go to Miss Defty, and the rest of you non-swimmers, go quietly to the shallow end and sit on the bench. I was very excited, but I would have to wait my turn.

Miss Rapp then gave her attention to the top group. She called the first girl forward.

"You are to jump in near the steps, and swim straight to the shallow end without stopping, and you are to stay by the wall."

The first girl jumped in and went right under. As soon as she surfaced, she started to swim to the shallow end. Miss Rapp walked along the side with a rope in her hand and holding a long pole. She held the pole with one end just in front of the swimmer, like dangling a carrot in front of a donkey. If a girl gave up before completing the length, and grabbed hold of the pole, Miss Rapp made a note of this on her clipboard and said, "Please go to Miss Defty's group."

I wondered if this would be the fate of June Rogers. June jumped in and started to swim. Miss Rapp dangled the pole in front of her for just a few yards and then said, "Good, keep going until you get to the end and then climb out," and then she turned her attention to the next girl. "Are you ready? Go."

When these tests were completed, Miss Rapp blew her whistle. "These girls are allowed to swim in the deep end," and she called out the names of the successful swimmers. "The rest of you listen very carefully. You are not allowed at any time to go beyond the blue line."

Now it was our turn. Miss Rapp came to the shallow end and spoke to the non-swimmers. "You are to climb down the steps, with your back to the water, and spread out to find a place on the rail."

It was icy cold, and it took my breath away.

"Jump up and down to get warm, hold the rail. Now wet your face – and rest. Put your face in the water and blow bubbles. Good. Now, this time ...." Her tone of voice suggested that she was going to tell us how to swim. I listened eagerly. "Now, this time I want you to jump up and down three times, holding the rail, and on the third one, you are to go right under! Well done! Now, we'll try that again and see if anyone can sit on the bottom."

I went down – the water went up my nose and I sat on the bottom. "Very good, June," she said when I came up. I wanted to be the best, but I was beginning to realise that learning to swim was going to take a bit longer than I had expected.

She blew her whistle and told us to get out, and to put our towels round our shoulders. She called June Rogers over and spoke to her and June went to the deep end.

"Now, I want you all to watch. Are you ready June? – Go!"

We stood along the side of the pool to watch this demonstration. June jumped in and swam past us all, demonstrating a beautiful, relaxed and perfectly symmetrical breaststroke. The thrust from her strong leg kick made her glide forward in a streamlined position. She made it look easy and graceful. I was filled with admiration and envy, and had a new respect for this hitherto unsporty classmate.

"Thank you June," said Miss Rapp, "Well done. Now, will those girls whose names I have called to be allowed to swim in the deep end, please report to me in the gym on Monday afternoon to get your 'First Stripe'."

The 'First Stripe' was just a piece of white tape to be sewn on our woollen costumes. It was nothing spectacular but it was a badge of achievement! I envied those girls and admired them, and I could think of nothing I wanted more than my 'First Stripe'.

"Now I want you all to get changed very quickly," said Miss Rapp, "and make sure you don't leave anything behind in the changing rooms."

In the cubicle I dried myself and started to dress. I thought about the lesson. I was quite pleased with what I had done – I think I was the only one in my group who had sat on the bottom, and Miss Rapp had praised me. I hadn't expected it to be so cold and I was disappointed that progress was going to be so slow.

I could hear the chatter of my classmates in the other cubicles and then I heard one of them saying: "Hey, did you see? June Matthews can't swim!"

I felt mortified. Embarrassed! Humiliated! I should have shouted back 'Of course I can't swim – I've never been in a swimming pool before. They didn't have one in Baldock, so when could I have learned to swim?' But I said nothing. I hadn't recognised the voice of the girl who had publicly denounced me. It's horrid when girls talk about you behind your back and this was cruel. I was Games Captain and now the centre of their ridicule. Would they have voted for me if they had known? Probably not. I wondered if Rosemary was regretting having nominated me. I'd let her down and I'd let myself down. June Rogers had won the respect of the class, and I, through no fault of my own, had lost it. I walked back to Valley Road with Billie, but I didn't feel like talking.

"You're quiet," she said, "what's the matter?"

"I'm freezing cold and starving hungry," was all I could think of to explain my mood. I felt ashamed of myself and very angry because it was not my fault.

Now I had a problem, and I would have to do something about it. Next day was Saturday and the pool would be open at 10 o'clock. 'Everybody had to have a first day,' I reasoned with myself. 'There must be a day when you swim for the first time. June Rogers couldn't swim when she was born, so she must have had a 'first day', and my 'first day' will be tomorrow. I made a pledge with myself. I would get to the pool at 10 o'clock, and I would not get out until I could swim – even if it meant missing lunch, which would make Mrs Cuss very angry.

Mrs Cuss put my towel and costume out to dry.

"Do you think my costume will be dry by the morning? I want to go again. I can't swim and I want to learn."

"I don't know," she replied, "It's woollen and it's very thick."

Next morning, after breakfast I packed my bag, feeling very excited. This was The Day. "I'm going to learn to swim today!" I confided in Mrs Cuss, and off I went to the pool.

I was there before it opened and had to wait to buy my ticket. There was nobody else there. I changed into the cold damp costume, which stuck to my legs as I tried to pull it on. I put on my hat and made my way to the shallow end. The pool was empty and there was nobody on the poolside, supervising. I went down the steps, backwards as Miss Rapp had instructed.

I thought I knew what to do, but was scared to do it, so I needed to break it down into small stages. I jumped up and down and went under. If I went under when I was trying to swim, it would be the same but my legs would be behind me, so I held onto the steps and went under, stretching my legs out behind me. Then I tried that again, letting go of the steps for a second, and grabbing them again. I found that I was quite near the surface of the water.

I knew what I had to do. You just had to lie on the water and paddle yourself along with your arms, and kick with your legs. I had seen the others doing it and they stayed up. Even if I went under, it wouldn't really matter because I could shut my eyes and hold my breath.

I leaned towards the bar and, just as I was about to try it, at the very last moment my left leg came forward and my foot went on the bottom. I tried again, but every time I tried, my left foot came to my rescue to save me. I was scared to try it. 'This is silly' I said to myself, 'you haven't come all this way to keep hopping on one foot, and you can't go home until you've done it, so you might as well do it now and get it over with. You'll have to try it and see what happens and the sooner you do it, the sooner you can go home!'

I decided to try one stroke. I stood about a yard from the steps. 'Here goes' I thought, 'and no hopping on one foot!' I held my breath and screwed my eyes tightly and launched myself on to the water.

I thrashed away blindly, doing quick circular movements with my arms, expecting to reach the steps in one, or at the most two strokes. It took me at least six strokes before I felt the steps and I grabbed them with relief. Six strokes! I was hardly moving but – I was swimming.

Each time I tried, I added a new challenge. First I tried opening my eyes, just for a second. Then I tried keeping them open. It was not so frightening with my eyes open because I could see the steps, and with my head above water I could snatch a quick breath. Now I knew there wouldn't always be the steps to grab hold of when I wanted to stop, so I swam towards the steps and tried to stop without touching them. They were there, within grabbing distance, if things went wrong. I practised this a few times until I was sure that I could stop and start without using the steps. Then came the big moment. I stood with my back to the steps and went off across the width, and stopped half way across.

I was feeling quite elated and pleased with myself, but I needed to breathe regularly. I was still holding my breath most of the time, and snatching a quick breath when I dared. Gradually it improved. If I could do a whole width, I could be in Miss Defty's group, and with that incentive I swam my first width. I could do it. Today had been my day. I could swim. And now, if I wanted to, I could go home. I stayed a bit longer to practise and it was getting easier.

At this point, I was joined by another swimmer. A man came and dived in at the deep end and swam a length.

"I've just learned to swim," I told him, "and I can do a width. Watch me." I was swimming with my chin stretched forward and my head back to keep the water off my face.

"Try swimming sidestroke," he suggested, "you'll find it much easier to breathe."

He was right. Sidestroke was easy and I soon got the feel of a strong scissor kick which gave much more propulsion. Then I had an idea.

"At school, we have to jump in the deep end and swim a length. Would you swim next to me while I try, please?" and he agreed. "I'll just try jumping in first, near the steps." I had noticed how quickly all the girls surfaced yesterday and thought it must be easy.

"When your feet touch the bottom, push up hard." I did that, but came up choking and spluttering from the water which had gone up my nose.

"Try holding your nose next time," he said. After that there was no problem. I jumped in, swam a length on my side with him swimming next to me. I knew that all I had to do now, was do this alone and I would be ready for Miss Rapp's test for my 'First Stripe'.

"I think I'll be all right to try it on my own now. Thank you for helping me."

I jumped in again and swam to the shallow end and climbed out.

"I've got to go now. I mustn't be late for my lunch. Thank you and goodbye."

"Goodbye," he replied, "and good luck!"

I went home, very happy and pleased with my morning's work. I had made myself do it, and I thought Mrs Cuss would be impressed.

"I can swim," I announced as soon as I got back. "I can jump in the deep end and swim a length."

"Don't tell lies," said Mrs Cuss.

"I can. I really did it. There was a man there and he told me to hold my nose when I jumped in, and he showed me how to do sidestroke, and he swam next to me the first time, to look after me, and then I did it on my own."

"Well then," she argued, "you must have been lying this morning when you said you couldn't swim!"

You just couldn't win with Mrs Cuss. I didn't try to explain that there had been no pool in Baldock, so I had never been before. It wasn't worth arguing with her. She should have believed me because I was telling the truth. I knew she didn't like me. She had said I had been lying before, about taking my pen into the bedroom, and even when we found out that it was the ribbon, she didn't say she was sorry. She thought I was a liar and I hated her.

I didn't tell anybody else about my visit to the pool on Saturday. I was wondering what I should say to Miss Rapp next lesson, to explain that I wanted to do my swimming test, but there was no problem. She started the lesson by saying, "Those girls who were excused swimming last week or were absent and want to swim a length, please go to the deep end." I just joined them and took my turn. She didn't ask me why I had been with the non-swimmers the previous week. She may have forgotten, or she may have assumed that I was in the wrong group by mistake. She may have thought that I hadn't been listening, or was, perhaps, a bit nervous.

It was unimportant. What was important was that I had earned my 'First Stripe', and joined June Rogers and the other competent swimmers in the deep end. Nobody in my class questioned me about this apparently miraculous improvement, and I didn't hear anyone in the changing rooms afterwards, saying 'Hey, did you see, June Matthews can swim after all!'

I was just pleased that I had redeemed myself. I hadn't let Rosemary down, and I was now a worthy Games Captain.

On my next visit home I told Mum I could swim. She was pleased, but she did not seem to be very surprised. "Mum, if I said to you that I couldn't swim, and that I went swimming on my own in an open air pool, and on the very same day, I jumped in the deep end and swam a length, would you have believed me?

"Oh yes," she said.

"Mrs Cuss didn't believe me. She said I was lying. Why would you believe that I could do all that in one day?"

"Because I know you, and I know how determined you are!"

202

And that was the big difference. Mrs Cuss did not know me. Nobody in Welwyn Garden City really knew me.

* * * * * * * * * *

Life with Mrs Cuss had not got off to a very good start. I don't think she wanted an evacuee and I can't blame her for that. It must have been very difficult to take a complete stranger into your home, especially someone from a totally different background.

It was not a matter of choice. Billeting officers would visit homes and decide how many evacuees could be accommodated, and of course, no attempt was made to find compatible placements. Mrs Cuss would probably have been better off with one of the fee-payers who would have felt at home in her show-house luxurious home. I was clearly from a working class family – a lower working class family, or even worse, a lower, non-working class family. With hindsight, I can understand how someone from her privileged background would look with suspicion upon someone from a lower social group. She may have equated my background with the criminal classes – the poor who lived by their wits and who were not to be trusted. She probably doubted my integrity, and certainly thought I was not to be believed.

At the time, I could make no such excuses for her. I could not understand why she should doubt my word. The only explanation I could think of was that she didn't like me, and I felt rejected. If she didn't like me then I didn't like her, and since I couldn't earn her respect or approval, there seemed to be no point in doing anything to please her.

The final straw came one Saturday at dinner. We had sausages, potatoes, cabbage and parsnips. The parsnips were boiled, and at first I thought they were potatoes. I had never had parsnips before and with my first mouthful, I thought it was a bad potato. It was soft and mushy with a strange unfamiliar sweet taste. I pushed them to the side of my plate and carried on eating the rest of the meal.

"I hope you're going to eat your parsnips," said Mrs Cuss, seeing quite clearly that I had no intention of doing so.

"I don't like them!"

"They're good for you."

"I don't like them," I repeated.

Mrs Cuss was watching me closely. I found a small piece of parsnip, almost hidden under the cabbage, and very carefully separated it with my knife and pushed it away to join the pile of parsnips on the edge of the plate. She was still watching me. I carefully pushed all of it right to the edge of the plate just to annoy her.

"I shall be very angry," she said, "if it ends up on the tablecloth."

I carried on eating the rest of the meal, keeping my eyes on the plate, not wishing to look at Mrs Cuss, but I could feel her watching me.

"It's wicked to waste food, you know. There's a war on."

I didn't need to be reminded. If we weren't at war I would be at home, and I wouldn't be expected to eat parsnips. All the same, I did feel guilty at wasting food and I thought of all the posters I had seen telling me not to waste anything.

Everything was in short supply; there was a world shortage. There were big pig bins for food – the pigs would eat anything, even if it was bad. Bones were collected separately as they could be used for making glue. Tins were saved, and silver paper and aluminium for making aeroplanes. I heard of one woman who was given a set of saucepans for a wedding present. Her husband heard the government appeal for unwanted saucepans, and thought the 'war effort' was more important than their own need. 'These could help to build an aeroplane,' he said, 'and I think we should let them go.' He then proceeded to crush them all, to prevent anyone else from rescuing them from the scrap heap for their own use.

The words 'WASTE NOT WANT NOT' went though my mind, and 'A clear plate means a clear conscience – don't take more than you can eat'. Did that mean that you were supposed to eat something that someone else had put on your plate even if you didn't like it? I thought it was a pity that Mrs Cuss didn't keep pigs or chickens. Nothing was wasted in Radwell.

I thought about my war effort and wondered if I should try to eat the parsnips. I had always tried to do all the things we had been told, and I wanted to help but I had never been in this position before. There seemed to be quite a lot of parsnips. Would it help if I ate half of it, I wondered, or would I have to eat it all? And even if I did eat it, I couldn't see how it would help us to win the war.

"If you don't eat your parsnips, you won't have any pudding," said Mrs Cuss, trying a different approach.

There's only one answer to that. "I don't want any

pudding," was my immediate response." Now that was a lie! I loved puddings but I wasn't going to be bribed. Well, it wasn't really a lie, because what I meant was 'I love puddings, but I am prepared to miss one rather than eat the parsnips,' and that was not a lie.

Mr Cuss had said nothing all this time. They had talked to each other, but he gave no indication of his views on the ongoing battle. I looked at him once and our eyes met. I felt sure he was on my side.

Mrs Cuss took their plates into the kitchen, leaving my plate in front of me. Mr Cuss and I looked at each other, but he said nothing. It was a friendly look but he clearly had no intention of getting involved. I believe he felt sorry for me.

Mrs Cuss returned with the pudding. One of my favourites – treacle sponge and custard. For a moment, I considered eating the parsnips quickly to earn my pudding, but they were cold now and I decided against it. I wondered whether to say 'May I leave the table, please?' but hoped that Mrs Cuss might relent and let me have some pudding – even if I couldn't have second helpings. Pigs might fly!

Mrs Cuss cleared the table leaving me facing the cold parsnips.

"You can sit there until you have eaten it all," she said, and with those few words I knew I was going to be the winner of this confrontation. I would sit it out.

How long, I wondered, would it be before they came looking for me? Possibly Monday or if not, Tuesday. They would wonder why I was not at school. They would come looking for me and find me still sitting at the table staring at a heap of cold parsnips.

I said nothing and pushed my plate away and moved my chair back a few inches. I crossed my legs and folded my arms slowly, knowing that my body language told her that I was prepared for a long, long wait. I looked up at the ceiling and out of the window. Perhaps if Mrs Cuss were to realise how determined I could be, she might just wonder if I had been telling the truth about learning to swim. I sat there for ages, but I knew that she would have to give in first.

I could hear her doing the washing up and hoped that she would soon want to wash my plate.

Eventually she returned and picked it up. "You are a very wicked girl," was all she said, and just to annoy her, I said as politely as I could, "May I leave the table, please?"

A few days later, I was sent for at school. The billeting officer told me I was to pack my bags and go back to the hostel. "And don't forget when you say goodbye to say 'Thank you for having me'."

No reason was given for moving me and none was needed. Mrs Cuss had obviously complained strongly about my behaviour and whatever she had said about me, they had believed. I did not think I had behaved badly. Nobody asked me what had happened, to hear my side of the story, and I couldn't have proved that I had not told lies, but if my teachers knew I was being sent back, they would think I was a 'difficult girl' and a 'problem'.

Well, I hadn't been difficult for four years with Auntie Edie and Uncle 'erbert, and I can't ever remember them being cross with me.

My friends at the hostel were pleased to see me, and I was very happy to be back with them again

BUZZ BOMBS AND ROCKETS

In wartime, both sides of the conflict try to keep one step ahead of their enemy. They are always designing new weapons, faster planes and bigger guns. They are developing more sensitive radar, and smarter intelligence, hoping to catch the enemy unawares. They must always expect the unexpected.

It landed in the middle of Russell Square on the bandstand. It was not a bomb, there was no shrapnel, but it had exploded. It looked more like a plane but it wasn't the right shape. The depth of the crater, which it had made, showed evidence of its lethal potential. We gathered round, trying to make sense of it. There was some speculation initially, that it was a plane flown by a suicide pilot, but this theory was soon discounted. It was eventually identified as the first of the rockets, the V1, usually referred to as doodlebugs or buzz bombs.

It was believed that they were launched from the northern coast of France, for the short journey across the channel. They were fired as rockets and were engine-assisted. The engines could be programmed to cut out when they had reached their targets, and they would then fall to the ground.

Some were intercepted and shot down by our fighter planes, and others were caught up in the heavy cables of the barrage balloons before they could reach their target but an estimated 2400 got through each carrying about 2000lbs of explosive. They travelled faster than traditional bomb-carrying planes so there was seldom time for an air-raid warning, but we knew when they were coming. They had an unmistakeable engine sound, with which we became all too familiar. And what was worse than listening to their motor, was the silence which followed when they stopped. At first the engine would falter briefly, and then continue spluttering intermittently for several seconds. We knew it was going to stop.

The silence that followed was unbearable. We knew that it was on its way down. The seconds seemed to be like hours and the silence of the engine was matched only by the silence on the ground. People stood still. Nobody spoke. We just waited. 'Please, not me,' we prayed. The anticipation, as we waited for the explosion, made them, in my opinion, the most sinister, terrifying weapon that we had to face.

As with all weapons, they could be developed and improved. The buzz-bombs, V1s, gave way to the rockets, the V2s. These were bigger, more accurate and more powerful, and were the first rockets to travel faster than the speed of sound. About 1300 were fired against London. Their trajectory was too high for fighter planes or barrage balloons and we had no warning at all of their approach. There was just a sudden explosion, and the damage was much greater, but in many ways they were a great relief. If you heard a rocket explode you were lucky, you had escaped. If it hit you, you were unlucky, but you would not know much about it. Either way you had been spared that terrifying psychological torment of the V1s.

The buzz bombs might have caused less physical damage, but if the enemy had been aware of the fear and trauma which they had created, and the detrimental effect they had on morale, they would not have wasted their efforts in replacing them with a weapon which was far less frightening.

* * * * * * * * *

About a week after the arrival of the first doodlebugs,

news was coming in about a successful attack and advance by the allies, which would change the course of the war. The good news was not fully appreciated at the time, particularly by those under rocket attack, because it seemed then as though Hitler had the upper hand.

'Operation Overlord' had been planned over many months with the cooperation of our allies. The plan was to invade France and eventually to liberate it. It involved five infantry divisions – two American, two British, and one Canadian. More than 130,000 troops were to land on 50 miles of the beaches of Normandy. In May, over 6,000 ships and landing-craft transported nearly a quarter of a million vehicles and more than half a million tons of supplies. This exercise required the construction of artificial harbours and floating piers.

Hitler was beginning to suspect that an invasion was being planned, but assumed that it would be opposite Dover. A phantom army had been created in that area, giving the Germans false radio information, and by the time they realised that this was a bluff, they were too late to prepare for our landing.

The invading forces left England from eleven different bases on the south coast simultaneously, stretching from Falmouth to Dover. They landed at 6 am on June 6th 1944 – 'D' Day.

General Montgomery, under Eisenhower, was the Commander of the Ground Invasion Forces, and with the Allies, moved southwards in the following weeks to liberate Paris on August 26th 1944. General De Gaulle led the victorious march triumphantly along the Champs Elyses.

Inevitably casualties were high – the Americans alone suffered a loss of nearly 10,000 lives, but D-Day has been recognised as an historic turning point in the history of Word War 2 – 'the beginning of the end' – and the major contributors from the Allied Forces were signatories to a commemorative certificate.

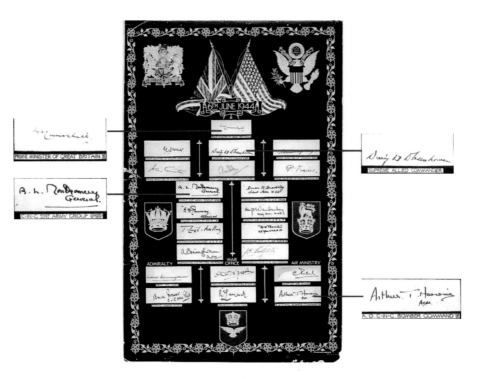

The news bulletins talked of successes, advances and achievements. Spirits rose and we began to sense victory. We had the enemy on the run. It was now only a question of time and our thoughts turned to going home. Again we sang along with Vera Lynn:

> *When the lights go on again*
> *All over the world,*
> *And the boys are home again*

All over the world.
And rain or snow is all
That may fall from the skies above,
A kiss won't mean goodbye
But hello to love.

When the lights go on again
All over the world,
And the ships will sail again
All over the world.
Then we'll have time for things
Like wedding rings.
And free hearts will sing,
When the lights go on again
All over the world.

MENSTRUATION

It was during one of my weekends in London that I was ill. I didn't know at the time, whether it was something I had eaten or something I had caught, but I was definitely very ill. It was on a Saturday night soon after I went to bed. I got up and went into my mother's room, and said quietly, "Mum, I've got the belly-ache and I think I'm going to be sick!" She got up and we went into the kitchen, and she put two chairs in front of the dying embers of the fire, with the bucket between us. "You look very pale," she said, putting her hand on my forehead. I felt worse than pale, I felt decidedly grey. I sat, leaning forward, staring at the bottom of the bucket, waiting, waiting ……. but the feeling of nausea passed, and for a little while, I felt better. Then it came back, the dizziness, the pain and the discomfort, the sweating and the feeling that I was about to be sick. I stared again at the empty bucket, rocking backwards and forwards, trying to ease the pain, but again, nothing happened and the intensity of the pain subsided.

The fire was nearly out, and although I had put a jumper on, I was beginning to feel cold. Mum put a blanket round my shoulders, and she put her arm round me. This was something new and it was good. I couldn't remember Mum ever putting her arm round me before. She was a very loving mother, but cuddles were not part of our agenda. We were not that kind of family. When we met or parted, or said goodnight, we always exchanged kisses, but they were very restrained. Just a quick peck on the lips. The deep love behind those quick kisses was there, but very much under control. No surrounding arms, or hugs, or outward show of emotion. Mum's love for us was never in question. She was an angel, a saint, and her every action spoke of her love for us. She was, without doubt, the best mother in the world. But tonight, she had put her arm round me and it was wonderful. It was worth being ill to enjoy this moment.

"Do you want a hot water bottle?" she asked.

"No, I'm not cold," I replied, "I'm all right." I would have loved a hot water bottle, but if she took her arm away, she might not put it back. The pain and the nausea returned at intervals but the bucket remained empty. We must have sat there for two hours or more until finally I came to the conclusion that I was not going to be sick. "I think I'll be all right to go back to bed now," I said, "but I'll take the bucket with me just in case."

Mum boiled the kettle and filled the hot water bottle and I got back into bed very quietly without waking the boys. She tucked me in and kissed me goodnight, and exhausted from this experience, I slept until late the next day.

When I woke, the colour had returned to my cheeks, and the memory of Mum's arm around me was something I have never forgotten.

Exactly three weeks later, again on a Saturday night, I was back in the dormitory at Valley Road. I woke with the same crippling pain and the strong feeling of nausea. I was ill again, but this time it was different, and I felt very uncomfortable. I got my torch from the side of the bed and shone it under the bedclothes. My pyjamas and the sheets were soaked in blood. I had started my periods. This was awful. Why hadn't this happened three weeks ago, when I was with Mum?

I had joined the band of girls who were excused swimming once a month. I had always viewed this group with mixed feelings. There was, undoubtedly, a strong feeling of envy. They had a certain status. They were maturing, and had a knowledge and experience that younger girls could not imagine. On the other hand, they had to miss a quarter of their swimming lessons, and sometimes they were excused gym or netball, and that seemed such a waste of the best lessons of the week. I thought I knew all about it, but I didn't think it would be like this. I knew you had to wear a sanitary towel, but no one had prepared me for the stomach-ache. Was it always going to be so unpleasant? I discovered later that it was, but on this, my first time, I didn't really know what to do. I didn't have any sanitary towels and was totally unprepared.

Looking back, I am amazed that I was so completely unprepared for what was such a totally predictable situation. All the grown-ups in my life had let me down. Mum didn't guess, because there was no bleeding. I should have said to her next morning, 'Mum, I wasn't sick last night so it couldn't have been food poisoning, and I'm all right this morning, so I'm not ill. Can you think of any reason why, just before my thirteenth birthday, I should feel sick and have the belly ache which kept coming and going for two or three hours?'

And what about the warden? She was in charge of a house full of girls, all of whom were likely to have to confront this experience, sometime or other, while they were in her care. The least she could have done was to have made sure we had some towels ready, and a belt to hold them up. At school, there was no pastoral care programme, such as was introduced in the 'seventies, and I suppose my form teacher would have considered it to be more the responsibility of the warden.

And what about the government and the local authorities? They had been responsible for taking us away from our families and putting someone else in *loco parentis*. Did it not occur to anybody that it would be a traumatic and distressing experience, for which we needed preparation and guidance? The thinking seemed to be that it was quite natural, it would happen to every girl, and she would learn all about it when it happened. And when it happened to me I realised that I was on my own. Growing up was not always going to be easy but nobody else could do it for you.

* * * * * * * * * *

Living in the hostel was like being at boarding school except that lessons were not held on the premises. You were with your friends, twenty-four hours a day. You walked to school with them, went back and had meals together, and helped each other with homework and then shared a dormitory for the night. Secrets and confidences were shared and close bonds established. And I loved it. If I had spent all my time at Welwyn Garden City in the hostel, it would have been two more happy years as an evacuee. But it was not to be.

Sadly, hostel placements were temporary, and you were moved out when a foster home was found. Billie had been placed with a family on the other side of town and eventually another home was found for me. I was to go to Mrs Brown, even farther away, past the Campus.

Mrs Brown was about 30 years old and lived with her little boy of about two in a modern house. It was comfortable and homely, but not posh like Mrs Cuss.

There was no Mr Brown. They were divorced! When I had asked Auntie Edie what the word 'divorce' meant, she had replied, "Oh, you don't want to worry yourself about words like that." I knew now what it meant and I didn't like it. Divorce was bad. When you got married, you were supposed to stay together forever, especially if you had children.

Divorce laws have changed over the years, and have been simplified. Attitudes have changed and people have become more understanding and sympathetic, but in those days it was quite difficult to get a divorce. There was a stigma attached to it and it was something to be ashamed of.

I didn't feel comfortable with Mrs Brown, and to make matters worse, she had a boyfriend. He wasn't there all the time, but when he came, he often stayed the night and slept in her room. I felt uneasy in their presence but I couldn't do anything about it and I had to make the best of it.

Mrs Brown was quite easy to get on with and not very strict about what time I got home in the evening, nor about bedtime.

If I'd been out with Billie who had to be home by eight o'clock, I would walk home with her first, and stay with her till the last minute. It was often half past eight before I got home, but Mrs Brown didn't seem to mind. I was allowed as much freedom as I wanted.

One day she confronted me.

"Do you ever do anything wrong when you're out?" she asked. Well, nobody's perfect, and sometimes we did things we were not supposed to do and hoped we wouldn't be found out. Now I was being challenged and I had to own up and hope I wouldn't get into trouble.

"Well," I said nervously, "Billie and I climbed the fence behind the Backhouse Rooms, and we got into the garden and stole some apples."

"No," said Mrs Brown, "I didn't mean things like that. I mean, do you ever do anything wrong with boys?" I knew what she meant and I was shocked to be asked such a question.

"No, I don't know any boys," I replied and if I had known any, I would certainly not have done anything like that.

I hoped that one day I would meet a nice boy and we wouldn't do anything until we were married. And then we would stay married, like Mum and Dad. I wouldn't want to get divorced. I thought it was because she was divorced and let her boyfriend spend the night with her, that she thought of such things. What sort of person did she think I was? I didn't want to live with someone who thought so badly of me. I was very unhappy and felt I couldn't stay there.

There was nobody I could talk to, to tell them what I had been accused of – because that's what it was. She believed I had done the things she was asking me about.

This was the second foster home in Welwyn Garden City which wasn't working out. The school would think I was a difficult pupil with problems. Where else could they send me? Nobody else would want me if I was always a problem. What could I do? I couldn't ask for another billet, and I couldn't stay with Mrs Brown. I was going home.

RUNNING AWAY

I decided to go back to London. Mum was back home and it was the only place to go. I wished I had stayed there when I had gone home for the weekend. I wasn't due for another weekend at home for quite a while and I couldn't wait that long. I just had to get away.

I packed my bags and my satchel, and went to the station. "Half to King's Cross, please – single."

I looked out of the train window and saw the school up on the hill, and the open-air swimming pool where I had learned to swim. I hoped I was seeing them for the last time.

As we approached North London, I looked out on the other side to see the public house which sold Uncle 'erbert's beer, 'SIMPSONS BALDOCK ALES' - painted on the wall, and I thought of my happy days in Radwell.

Mum was surprised to see me. "I'm not staying there any more. I hate it. I've come home and I'm not going back."

I couldn't really explain how I felt. Mrs Brown hadn't actually accused me of anything. She had only asked me a question, but

I knew what she was thinking. And people wouldn't understand how I felt about the divorce and her boyfriend. It seemed too complicated.

"What's gone wrong?" asked Mum.

"Oh, it's everything. I hate it and I'm not going back." I really wanted to talk to Mum, but I'd been away for five and a half years and although she was still my Mum, in some ways she was like a stranger.

"Do they know you've come to London?" Mum asked.

"I don't know and I don't care."

Of course, it wasn't long before they realised I'd gone. They contacted Mum to check that I was with her, and told her to take me to our London school in Stamford Hill. I was summoned to see Miss Barton, who spent half her time in the London school. It was a long journey from Herbrand Street – on the underground, Piccadilly Line, from Russell Square to Manor House; then on No. 653 trolley bus to Stamford Hill. This would be the journey I would have to make every day.

The school was an imposing red brick building with a bell tower, near a busy road junction. We were led through a magnificent oak-panelled hall with parquet flooring and a beautiful stained glass window. In front of the window was the platform, with stairs leading up to it on both sides, and the back wall was covered with large organ pipes, much bigger than in All Saints Church in Radwell.

There were classroom doors on both sides of the hall, and between them, photographs of stern-looking, retired headmistresses.

We were shown into Miss Barton's office, and she

was sitting there looking even more stern and severe than her predecessors.

"Mrs Matthews, would you like to sit down? I'm sorry you've had all this worry. June has been very inconsiderate in causing everybody so much anxiety."

She turned to me – of course, I had to remain standing. "June, do you realise how selfish and thoughtless you have been?"

"Yes," I answered quietly.

"Yes, Miss Barton," she prompted.

"Yes, Miss Barton," I repeated.

"And do you realise how much pain and anxiety you have caused us all, especially your Mother?"

"Yes," I replied, "………..Miss Barton."

"And we can't have girls like that in our school, can we?" Suddenly, I was frightened that I was going to be expelled.

"Can we, June?"

"No, Miss Barton." I couldn't imagine what Dad would say if I were to be expelled. He would never forgive me. He was so proud that I had won a place at a Grammar School. He would be very angry, and when he was angry I was very frightened of him. He did not punish us very often, but when he did, he was very heavy-handed. He had been angry with me before and that was bad enough but there had never been anything as serious as getting expelled.

I could feel the tears coming into my eyes. Perhaps I should explain to Miss Barton that I was frightened of what my father would do to me, and ask for another chance.

"Now," she continued, "Are you going to apologise to your Mother for all this distress you've caused her?" I saw a glimmer of hope that I might be able to remain at the school.

"I'm sorry, Mum," I said, turning to her.

"And you've also caused me - and the school - a lot of worry, haven't you?"

"Yes, Miss Barton. I'm sorry ……. Miss Barton."

"And can you give me an assurance that you will never behave so selfishly and dangerously again?"

"Yes, Miss Barton." I felt relieved that I would not have to face Dad's anger.

"Well, Mrs Matthews, if June has fully understood the error of her ways, and promises never to be so inconsiderate again, we would like you to take her back to Welwyn Garden City on Saturday, back to the hostel in Valley Road."

Thank goodness I was not being sent back to Mrs Brown. Nobody ever asked me why I had left – or why I was so unhappy there. I couldn't have explained it anyway, but at least they could have asked. You don't do things like that without a reason.

Back I went to 21 Valley Road, this time in Garage Dormitory. It wasn't the same. Most of my friends were now billeted out and I was getting restless.

PEACE

We were now in the Spring of 1945. The news was good and people were expecting the end of the war to be announced any day. After nearly six years we were winning the war, and we would be going back to London.

I hadn't realised until I was summoned to Miss Barton's office in London, that half the school was already there, and I wanted to join them. It was arranged that I should go to the

London school after the Easter holidays in April. Five weeks later, the armistice was signed, and May 5th was declared V.E. Day – Victory in Europe. It was to be another four months to V.J. Day (Victory in Japan), but we had won the war against Germany.

At last – it was the day we had all been waiting for. The church bells rang out and the lights went on again. People were singing and dancing in the streets and hugging each other. Horns and claxons were being sounded and flags were flying.

We walked along Holborn Kingsway to see the lights, and along the Strand to Trafalgar Square. There was nothing to do except to enjoy being there. You could talk to people you did not know and everybody was happy. We had waited a long time for this celebration and we were going to make most of it.

The crowds started to walk down The Mall towards Buckingham Palace. People were climbing on the Queen Victoria Memorial and others crowded up against the Palace gates and railings (still safely in place) chanting 'We want the King! We want the King!' The message got through and the big doors opened and the Royal Family appeared on the balcony with Winston Churchill. The people cheered and waved and the Royal Family waved back. Everybody was happy – well not everybody.

Sadly, for many, it was not a time for celebration. Thousands of families were homeless and many were not re-united, having lost members in the front line of action, or in the bombing. Nearly one hundred thousand civilians had been killed and over a quarter of a million servicemen did not return. Worldwide it has been estimated that more thirty million allies were killed during the war and to this figure, the losses of our enemies must be added to reach the final toll. For the bereaved families it was a time of sadness but at least now we all knew that there would be no more loss of life.

We were surrounded by the devastation from the bomb damage. London and the big cities would have to be rebuilt, but the mood was one of hope and optimism. A new life was to begin.

The Bluebirds must have flown over the White Cliffs of Dover, and we could now look forward to 'love and laughter and peace ever after'.

PART FIVE

'The Homecoming'

'.....the albatross about my neck was hung .....'

Samuel Taylor Coleridge
The Rime of The Ancient Mariner

At last the war was over, and it was good to be home. We had waited six years for this and we had won the war. There was an atmosphere of joy and euphoria everywhere you went, and people were happy and friendly.

The flat seemed very small, and it was dark and oppressive, but it was our home.

'And Junie will go to sleep,
In her own little room again!'

Well – it wasn't quite like that because I had to share a room with John, now sixteen, and Basil, eight, but I was back 'in my own little bed again'.

The boys weren't so lucky because they had to share a single bed. There was no room in the flat to put another bed. Our bedroom was so small that the two beds were side by side, with a gangway of about eighteen inches between them, but this was only a temporary measure until we moved.

We would be re-housed because we were overcrowded and then I would have a room of my own. Nothing could spoil our victory and our homecoming.

And there was so much to look forward to: a proper school where we could have all our lessons without carrying our books around with us all day; cloakrooms where we could hang our coats with cubby holes underneath to keep our plimsolls; and school dinners served on the premises instead of on the other side of town. It would all be so easy.

There were other things to look forward to. There would be street parties for all the children and, best of all, there was going to be a week of Victory Celebrations. This was going to be a major national event and would take a long time to organise, and so it would probably not be until the following year. It was something to look forward to.

With the exception of our overcrowded living accommodation, everything seemed perfect, and because of our ages and different sexes we were confident that our housing needs would be given priority. We would be top of the list.

The lady in the Housing Department shattered our hopes.

"I'm very sorry," she said sympathetically, "but you don't qualify to go on the list. We already have too many people to re-house."

"But I've got a teenage daughter sharing a small room with two boys," said Mother, "and we've got no running water in the flat and no toilet."

"I'm sorry," repeated the lady, "but at least you have somewhere to live. There are a lot of people with no home at all. Their houses have been bombed and we must find them somewhere first."

"Can we go on the waiting list for a place when you have re-housed the homeless?"

"No – at the moment the waiting list is only for those with nowhere to go. Come back again in about a year."

A year! It was an eternity. The flat seemed even smaller and darker and the facilities even more primitive. There was no washbasin in the house – not even a kitchen sink. Water was carried into the house in a jug from the tap on the public landing, and carried out again in the slop bucket, to be emptied down the public toilet – if it was not in use by our neighbours. A year! And it wasn't going to be a year until we could move, but a year before we could go on the waiting list. It was very depressing.

PUBLIC BATHS AND WASH-HOUSES

During my two years at Welwyn Garden City, I had become accustomed to the convenience of hot and cold running water and indoor toilets. Looking back, the five inches of bathwater that we had been allowed, seemed a real luxury. Now even a simple thing like washing hair became a major event – filling the jugs and the saucepans, boiling the water on the gas, and topping them up for the rinsing water. We had to put the enamel bowl on the stool and kneel in front of it. You had to move your head out of the way to dip a cup into the bowl to pour water over your head. At each stage, the bowl had to be emptied into the slop bucket which had to be taken out of the flat to be emptied.

Personal hygiene, particularly during menstruation, was even more difficult as there was no privacy in the flat. It was basically a choice between washing when Dad and the boys had gone out, or not washing at all.

One solution to this problem was an occasional visit on a Saturday morning to the Public Baths and Washhouse in Endell Street. It was about a mile away and it took the whole morning because it was always so busy. You bought your ticket and then sat in the waiting room, clutching your soap and towel for anything up to two and a half hours. As bathers came out of their cubicles, the attendant would go and give the bath a quick wipe round before shouting 'Next!'

You had to be as quick as possible because the queues went on all day. The water supply was controlled from the outside by a large angled iron key with a wooden handle which was carried around by the attendant. On one end was a square hole which would lock on to a large bolt outside each cubicle. Then the handle could be turned to open the hot or cold water, as required. The amount of water you had was at the discretion of the attendant. You could hear people calling above the partitions 'More cold in number 5, please' or 'More hot in number 3, please'.

If you were too slow in getting undressed and then found it too cold, and you called out for more hot water, back would come the reply, 'How long have you been in there? You can't top it up with more hot water.' Someone shouted, 'Come on, the war's over and I haven't even got five inches in Number 6.' Someone else shouted back, 'I'm all right – I had six inches last night!'

Some attendants were more helpful and co-operative than others. The plugs, like the taps, were controlled from the outside, and it was not unknown for them to pull your plug out before you had finished. This could be a problem if you were washing your hair in the bath as the water could disappear before you had finished rinsing it. On one occasion, I had to squat in the bath with my foot over the hole and splash the dwindling water frantically over my head. It was not an occasion to relax in the bath or wallow in the hot water, but it was wonderful to feel clean again.

* * * * * * * * * *

The weeks passed and the initial feeling of euphoria subsided. It was peacetime but it was going to take a long time to get back to normal.

Rationing continued, and was likely to remain a necessity for a long time in the future. Men and women from the Armed Services were being de-mobbed and trying to find their way back into 'Civvy Street'. Some wanted their old jobs back but there had been so much change in six years that many of the posts no longer existed. Where they did exist, it was natural for men to step back into them. Tate and Lyle issued this letter to its predominantly female workforce in 1945:

> "The Directors and Management wish to thank all employees for the manner in which they have cheerfully carried on during the last five and a half years. The war in Europe has been won and partial demobilisation will begin. Our first duty is to find jobs for those who are returning to us from the Forces. In many cases a returning man must displace someone, man or girl, who has been holding down the job during the war."
>
> Tate & Lyle, June 1945

Although this was considered to be fair and reasonable, women were not prepared to revert to the role that they had had in the 'thirties. They had been called upon to replace the male workforce and had shown themselves to be quite capable of doing the work. They had enjoyed the opportunity to develop their skills and had grown in self-confidence. They were not able to retain the posts of responsibility that they had held during the war, but neither were they prepared to accept the drudgery and humiliation they had experienced before.

Dad was in a similar position. He was working in the Civil Service on Temporary Grade, but was hoping to be confirmed as a permanent pensionable employee. For as long as he could continue working, even on a comparatively low wage, our days of appalling poverty were over. John was now sixteen and had left school and found employment with G.E.C. in Holborn. Things were going to be a lot easier. All we wanted was a bigger and better home.

* * * * * * * * * *

During the whole of the war, our country had been led by a coalition government, with members of all political parties working together for a common goal. Winston Churchill was a Conservative, but his war cabinet included people of ability from other parties. For example, Herbert Morrison (Labour Party) was the Home Secretary.

In times of war, they could forget their differences and co-operate with each other in the national interest.

Now that the war was over, a coalition government was no longer necessary and a General Election was planned for July. I had no understanding of politics and very little interest. My parents had no political allegiance and never expressed any views on the subject, so supporting one side or the other was rather like trying to guess the winner in the Oxford and Cambridge boat race and it would be nice to have supported the winning side.

Winston Churchill now seemed to be out of favour. He had everyone's full support at the beginning of the war, and we were confident that he would lead us to victory. He had done just that, but it had taken six long years, with many lives being lost and devastation in our cities. People had got tired of the shortages and the hardships and thought he had taken too long and he was now being described as a warmonger. People would now have the opportunity to vote to show their support for him, or otherwise.

At school, it was decided to hold a 'Mock Election'. Many of my school friends seemed to understand the issues, and meetings were held to select candidates for the different parties, who were then eager to publish their manifestos and proclaim their views.

Billie was a very strong supporter of the Labour Party. Her parents were Party Workers in Bethnal Green, and were actively involved in Local Government. Her mother was later to become the Mayor of Bethnal Green, with her eldest daughter, Dorothy, as her Mayoress.

I observed that in general, the fee-paying girls from wealthy backgrounds were supporters of the Conservative Party, whilst the scholarship girls from poor backgrounds were supporting the Labour Party. This trend was repeated outside school. Blue Tory stickers could be seen in the windows of big houses, whilst the red Labour stickers were prominent in the poorer looking homes and in the 'Buildings'.

My understanding of the issues was limited and my views very simplistic. It seemed to me that the Labour Party would put high taxes on the rich people, promising to improve the conditions for the poor. They promised us a National Health Service so that you would be able to see a Doctor or a Dentist – or even stay in hospital, without paying. It would all be 'free'. The rich people, of course, could already afford to pay. The Conservatives on the other hand, would not put up the taxes and wanted to keep things as they were. I did not know if a National Health Service would work but it seemed to be a good idea.

Mavis, as I would have expected, was a Labour supporter, but surprisingly so was Rosemary. She lived in a lovely big house and her parents seemed to be wealthy, but her political allegiance was entirely altruistic, certainly not based on self-interest.

We had political forums in the lunch-hours when we could ask questions and show our support, or heckle the opposition. It was great fun and we finally had our secret ballot. At our school, the Conservative candidates were elected but our electorate was not a representative cross-section of society. When the whole country voted, a Labour Government was elected with a huge majority and our new Prime Minister was Clement Atlee.

Soon after this we had local government elections. In the flat above us Mr Hampshire-Monk lived with his ageing mother. He was a candidate for the Conservative Party, with blue stickers in his window amidst a sea of red. I was surprised to learn that he was a Tory and even more so, that he was standing for election, but he was different from many of my neighbours. He was quiet, and very well dressed, and kept himself to himself. He never got drunk and did not seem to have any friends in the flats. He was certainly not a typical Peabody resident. And neither was I. We lived there, but did not want to. We had no choice. I did not know many people who, like us, were trying to get out. The Harrisons on the top floor were on the Housing list to be re-housed, but most people intended to stay and presumably liked living there. Well, I was different and I did not want people to think I was a typical Peabody tenant, and I could show my difference by supporting the Conservatives. I asked Mr Hampshire-Monk for a Tory sticker to put in our window but Dad would not let me put it up.

"Well, which party do you support?" I asked him.

"That's my business," he replied, and wouldn't tell me. "And if you take my advice," he continued, "you'll keep your opinions to yourself. When they come knocking on the door, canvassing for their candidates, I tell them all that I will vote for their man, and they all go away happy."

"Well, I'm going to be Conservative and help Mr Hampshire-Monk." I was not old enough to vote, but I could be a canvasser. The Party was delighted with my support. I put leaflets in all the doors in Peabody Buildings, and in Coram, Dickens and Thackeray Buildings on the other side of the road. There were seventeen blocks in all, each five stories high with no lifts, over twelve hundred stone stairs. And on the day of the election, I knocked on doors of our supporters again, urging them to vote. We lost, of course, but we had put up a good fight. I think Mr Hampshire-Monk must have been responsible for the letter I received from the Conservative Party Headquarters on headed notepaper, thanking me for my help and support and recognising the enormous effort I had made.

My support was a visible protest against living in Peabody Buildings. It would be a number of years before I was old enough to vote, by which time I had a more balanced view of the merits of the different political parties, but in 1946, I was a good little Tory worker.

STREET PARTIES AND THE VICTORY PARADE

The sadness caused by our inadequate living accommodation was alleviated from time to time by joyful events. There was a general air of happiness amongst the people, and even though rationing was to continue for some time, gradually the shelves began to fill up again. Sweets had been rationed but now there seemed to be greater choice.

The Government decided to take sweets off rationing from the beginning of the following month. Everyone went wild. The thought of being able to buy as many sweets and chocolates as you wanted was too much for most people, and on the first day people queued excitedly to make up for the years of deprivation. The shelves were soon empty. Those who had not joined in the rush could buy none. The shopkeepers could not get adequate supplies quickly enough, and as soon as a delivery arrived – they were gone. The Government realised that they had made an error of judgement – and sweet rationing was re-introduced the following month.

The euphoria continued and street parties were planned. We had ours in the yard. Trestle tables were brought in and covered with white paper tablecloths. Everywhere was decorated with red, white and blue bunting and flags. It was going to be a wonderful party. Everybody had to bring their own chair. Mothers made sandwiches with our favourite fillings – chocolate spread or peanut butter; they made cakes with icing on top, and jelly and blancmange, and there were chocolate biscuits and fruit trifles.

There was more than we could eat and it was wonderful. Afterwards there were the entertainments, Punch and Judy shows, a magician and games with prizes. Everybody was happy and had a wonderful time – well almost everybody. A friend of mine was not allowed to go to his street party. His father had been killed on active service during the war and his mother could see no reason to celebrate. My friend, then only four years old, could only look out of his window through the lace curtains with mixed emotions and watch the other children enjoying themselves. He recalls at the time feeling confused and bewildered. We were happy, and were celebrating our victory, relieved that there would be no more casualties, but for those who had suffered it was to be a hollow victory.

The celebration continued for the rest of the day, and when the children had finished, there was music and dancing for the adults.

We still had the big National event to look forward to and it was going to be in June the following year. They promised that it would be the biggest party the country had ever had. Everyone who had contributed to the victory would be represented in a big parade and it was certainly something to look forward to.

After about a year, we went again to the Housing Department. We sat for a long time in a small waiting room, hoping that when our turn came, we would be able to persuade the Housing Officer that we desperately needed to be rehoused. This time, we were interviewed by a man, who listened to our story and made notes. Then he filled in a form but explained that there were many people on the waiting list and that it took a long time to build new homes. He assured us that we were now on the list but he could give no indication of how long we would have to wait. We knew it would be years, rather than months, and the thought of it was very depressing – but at least we were now on the list!

* * * * * * * * * *

Mum promised to take Basil and me to the Victory Parade. We had been hearing about the Victory Celebrations on the wireless for weeks, and at last the day arrived – Saturday 8th June, 1946. It was now over a year since peace had been restored in Europe.

There would be entertainments in the afternoon and the evenings, for a week, with decorations, illuminations and

fireworks. All the important buildings and famous ships would be floodlit, and there would be music and dancing. It would be a wonderful week, starting with the big Victory Parade. We bought the 'Official Programme of the Victory Celebrations' for tuppence.

There were three processions in the Parade, each following a different route. The best place to go to see them all was the Mall, where there would be the 'Saluting Base'. We lived only a couple of miles away and made an early start to get a good view, in the front row. It was exciting to leave home at half past three in the morning. We looked enviously at other people who had had the foresight to bring chairs or cushions.

"We should have brought our cushions," Mum said, "Then we could have sat on them while we are waiting."

"I'll run back and fetch them," I volunteered, "It won't take me long." And back home I went, secure in the knowledge that Mum and Basil would keep our place.

There was an air of excitement as we waited for the parade to start. More and more people arrived, and we were pleased to be in the front row. We did not know any of the people around us, but everyone was friendly and happy, wearing colourful hats and waving Union Jacks.

At about 6.00 am we heard loud cheering farther up The Mall, and we could see flags being waved. We stood up to see what the excitement was about so that we could join in. It was the dustcarts. They came up The Mall making sure there was no litter on the Parade route. We were all in such a good mood that we cheered them enthusiastically. It was quite funny. The dustmen were laughing and one of them waved like the Queen. They were enjoying it as well. We still had quite a long while to wait but the big moment came at last.

'HIS MAJESTY'S PROCESSION' led the parade. The King, accompanied by the Queen, Princess Elizabeth and Princess Margaret, rode in the State Landau, escorted by a Captain's Escort of the Household Cavalry with the Royal Standard.

They left Buckingham Palace just after ten o'clock and paraded round Marble Arch, Oxford Street, Charing Cross Road, Whitehall and back to The Mall where we were waiting. We stood up as they were approaching, cheering and waving our flags as they rode past us in their magnificent open carriage. The King and Queen were truly majestic and the two Princesses looked beautiful. They were as happy as we were and they smiled and waved to us all the time. At the end of The Mall, near Buckingham Palace, they were installed at 'The Saluting Base' and were joined by the Chiefs of Staff at V.E. Day and V.J. Day and the Supreme Allied Commanders. We gave a special cheer to Winston Churchill and Montgomery who were easily recognised.

The 'MARCH PAST' consisted of two elements, the Mechanised Column and the Marching Column, each of which would follow its appointed route to the Saluting Base. As the Mechanised Column could move much faster, it was able to cover a greater distance, giving more people an opportunity to see it.

It started at Regent's Park, and went along Euston Road and through the City and Aldgate to Tower Hill crossing the River Thames at London Bridge. It then paraded South London through Newington Butts and Kennington Oval, returning across Vauxhall Bridge. From there, it went along Millbank to Parliament Square and Whitehall, and through Admiralty Arch to The Mall. Everything on wheels was in the Mechanised Column: police Motor Cycle Patrols; Despatch Riders of all the Armed Services, Ambulances, Mobile Sick Bays, Jeeps, Fire Engines, Ammunition Carriers, Radar vehicles and Bridge Laying Tanks; there were things we'd never heard of, but we knew they must have made an important contribution to the victory, so we cheered them all.

Civilian Services were well represented: Civil Defence rescue vehicles; blood transfusion vans; Church Army mobile canteens and an Insulated Meat van; there were Farm Tractors and a Mobile Telegraph Office. There were over two hundred groups represented in the Mechanised Column and all were greeted with waving flags and cheers.

The Marching Column could not cover such a great distance, so it stayed north of the river, marching from Marble

Arch to the Saluting Base in The Mall and then on to Hyde Park Corner.

All the Allied Forces were represented, followed by the Dominions, all with their Military Bands. The music was wonderful. As one band faded into the distance, the next could be heard approaching. Between them we cheered Rescue Dog Handlers, with their dogs, The Red Cross, Nurses, Midwives and Civil Defence Wardens. And of course, there were horses of the Household Cavalry and the Royal Horse Guards and all the Brigades of Guards.

It was a colourful, exciting and noisy parade followed by a Fly-Past. The heavy bombers flew over, and the fighter aircraft, and as the last plane flew over, we knew it was time to pick up our cushions and go home.

Before returning, we followed the surge of people up The Mall to Buckingham Palace, where we noticed that the magnificent black iron gates and railings with gold tops were still safely intact. They had not been required as scrap iron to build aeroplanes!

We stood outside the gates chanting 'We want the King, we want the King!' An enormous cheer went up as the doors opened and the Royal Family appeared on the balcony to wave to us.

That was not the end of the Day's celebrations. There were afternoon entertainments in all the big London Parks with music and dancing and Punch and Judy shows.

In the evening there was more music and dancing, and searchlight displays. These were really interesting, and you could see how the searchlights worked together to isolate enemy aircraft. They had RAF planes flying overhead. One of the searchlights swept backwards and forwards across the sky, like a windscreen wiper, until it caught the plane in its beam. The searchlight would then move slowly, following the plane's path in the sky. Another searchlight, from a different base, would then join in, shining its light slowly down the first beam, until it found the plane. Both searchlights could then track the plane, and you could see it clearly where the beams of the two searchlights crossed. If this had been an enemy aircraft, it could be attacked by fighter planes, or from the ground below. Sometimes there were three searchlights tracking a plane. Enemy planes were forced to drop their bombs before reaching their targets, which may have been munitions factories or railway junctions, and they would turn for home, hoping to escape. If they could be shot down as well, they would not be able to return the next night with another deadly load.

It must have been terrifying to see the searchlights at work during the war, in the blackout, but as part of the Victory Celebrations, it was very exciting, surrounded by aquatic fireworks, illuminations and music.

For the whole of the following week, London was a festival of music, light and colour. Flags were flying everywhere representing all the Services, the Dominions, the Colonies and fighting Allies. We had won the war and it was good to be alive. Not everyone, of course, was in the mood to enjoy the celebrations. Many were mourning the loss of relatives killed in action or in the bombing, and thousands were homeless. It would take years to repair the damage and to build new homes, but at least the hostilities had ended and there would be no more casualties. That was something to celebrate.

CAMPING

Teenagers are never the easiest people in the world to live with, and they seldom see eye to eye with their parents. For us, it was even more difficult and turbulent. I had left my family as a little girl of seven, and returned as an independent teenager, and in many ways my parents were strangers.

Dad had never really shown much interest in bringing up his children, but Mum had always taken the responsibilities of parenthood very seriously. She was a wonderful mother, and I loved her very much – as long as she didn't think that now she could tell me what to do. She tried a couple of times, always speaking gently and politely.

"Don't you think it's time you got ready for bed now, dear?"

"I'm not tired yet," I replied, "I'll be going soon."

Or on another occasion: "Haven't you got any homework to do this weekend?"

"I learned my French verbs on the train."

"What time will you be back this evening?"

"I don't know – I'll have a look at the clock when I get home, and then I'll let you know."

This cheeky sort of reply always made us both laugh – Mum appreciated my sense of humour – but I was making it quite clear that I would not accept her authority over me. She learned very quickly that I was quite easy to get on with as long as I was left to my own devices, so we jogged along quite peacefully.

It was difficult to have a normal close relationship after a separation of six years, but what made it even worse were our miserable living conditions which were causing so much unhappiness.

"This place is a dump," I complained, "I can't bring anybody here." I couldn't discuss it with anybody else, so it was always poor old Mum who had to listen to my complaints. "It's like a pigsty here, in fact it's not good enough for pigs."

Mum loved us, and wanted us to be happy, and it must have hurt her so much to see our suffering, and to know she could do nothing about it. She did all she could to make us happy, she cooked us wonderful meals in difficult circumstances, and she would make sacrifices to give us what we wanted. We were always clean and tidy when we went to school – and even that was difficult to achieve. Washing our clothes was obviously a problem without running water, but in addition to that, we had no electricity in the flat. This meant, of course, that we could not have an electric iron, and that all the pressing had to be done with a flat iron. We had two of these with the weight stamped on them, one of eight pounds and the other seven. They would have to be heated on the gas stove with no way of checking the temperature. The handles were an integral part of the iron, so these would get hot as well, and it was always necessary to hold them with an oven glove. There was no control over the temperature, it was entirely guesswork and experience. Mum used to pick up the iron and hold it with the flat surface one or two inches away from her face. She could feel the heat, and tell whether it was the right temperature. While one of the irons was in use, gradually losing its heat, the other would be back on the gas. In spite of these difficulties, our school clothes were washed regularly, and I was always proud of my well-groomed appearance.

Another difficulty for Mum was keeping the flat clean. Without electricity we could not have a vacuum cleaner and she was frequently on her knees scrubbing the floor. The beds were so close together that it was not easy to get a broom under them so I doubt if she could reach the corners. I remember that I often woke with little spots of blood on the sheet and pillow and thought I must have scratched a spot in my sleep. It was years before I realised that these were the tell-tale signs of bed bugs. I am glad I did not know this at the time.

Mum always did her best for us but she knew we were unhappy. Once she said to me, "I know you don't like it here, and it's not very nice for you, but this is the first real home I have ever had. I was very grateful to come here."

And she wasn't just referring to her married life. She had been born in 1909, and was illegitimate, which in those days was a great stigma. Her mother was a kitchen worker in one of the big country estates and lived in the servants' quarters. She had no facilities for looking after a baby, so Mum was placed in foster homes, and throughout her childhood she was moved from home to home, experiencing cruelty and exploitation.

At the age of twelve, having had no real education, she followed in her mother's footsteps and went into service. She worked as a servant until she was eighteen when she met my father, who was nearly sixteen years her senior. She soon became pregnant, and married Dad three months before John was born.

And even when she was married, she didn't have a proper home of her own until she moved to Peabody. I feel guilty and ashamed now at the way I behaved towards her during those miserable years. I didn't really appreciate what a rotten life she'd had, and I wish I had realised then that it was difficult for her as well in those squalid conditions. All she wanted was to love and care for her family, and she did her best to do this.

We did have some happy times, of course, and I think she knew how much I loved her, but I wish I had put my arms round her sometimes, and said 'I love you, Mum.'

I am glad that in later years we were able to talk freely about the difficult times and to speak openly of our love for each other. I told her what a good sport she had been and reminded her of some of the happier times we had had.

One of those memorable events occurred in 1946, when Basil had his ninth birthday.

"There's only one thing I want," he said, "I want a tent."

"A tent? What do you want a tent for?"

If he'd asked for a bike or a pair of roller skates, that would have made sense, but there was not a blade of grass anywhere to be seen near Peabody Buildings, and the local park-keepers would not welcome a tent on their precious little bit of grass.

"I want a tent," he repeated, "A bivouac."

Mum always tried to give us what we wanted and Basil got his bivouac. He was very pleased, of course, but surprise, surprise, he wanted to use it!

"Let's go camping!" I said, "I know, let's go to Windsor!" We bought a groundsheet and two sleeping bags and took a few useful bits and pieces – a thermos flask, a bottle-opener, a tin opener and some cutlery. John stayed at home with Dad and the three of us caught the Windsor train from Paddington. We stopped at a local shop to buy some provisions and wandered through the town looking for somewhere to camp for the night.

"Let's go down to the river bank," I suggested, "There's bound to be some grass there."

We were in luck. There was an island, which was

accessible by bridge, where we thought we would be safe and undisturbed. It was an ideal place to pitch the tent. The bivouac was very small. It was about six feet by four feet six inches, the size of a double bed, and only about three feet high in the centre. It was going to be a tight fit but we were used to being overcrowded.

We had no cooking facilities, but Mum had the hot thermos of tea. Supper was pork pies, tomato and bread, with a banana to follow. It was quite exciting bedding down for the night, even though the ground was very hard.

Breakfast was baked beans straight from the tin, and bread with lemonade to drink.

"Let's go swimming," I said. I was quite a strong swimmer and I had taught Basil to swim the previous year. Mum was terrified as she watched us get into the water because we were very close to the weir. There was a board saying 'DANGER – WEIR' just a little way from where we were swimming, but Mum knew that it would be no good arguing with me.

During the day we visited the castle and then wandered through the town looking for No. 7 Russell Street, which was one of the many homes where Mum had been fostered as a child. She and her younger brother Reg, also illegitimate, had lived there with Mrs Pearce who fostered a number of unwanted children. Mum recalled that she was older than the other children there, and as the only girl she was frequently kept away from school to look after the boys.

Back on our island, as we prepared for our second night, we had an unexpected visit from a policeman.

"And what are you doing here?" he asked, "This is private land. You're not supposed to be here. Mum seemed quite worried, as she was very law-abiding and thought we would be prosecuted, but I thought we could talk our way out of it

"Well, we couldn't find anywhere else to pitch our tent. He had it for his birthday. He's nine now, and there's no grass near Peabody Buildings in London, and we're going home tomorrow anyway."

While I was talking, the policeman had been looking at our facilities – or lack of them. He was almost smiling as he looked at the tent and asked, "And do you all sleep in there?"

"Yes, it's just about big enough, and we fold up our clothes to make a pillow."

"And you say you're going home tomorrow?"

"Yes, because we've got to go to school on Monday."

"Well, I shall be round again tomorrow," he promised, "so just make sure I don't see you again."

"Oh, thanks, we'll be gone, and we won't leave our baked bean tins or any rubbish, so no one will ever know we've been here."

"Good," he said, "and I hope you sleep well." And then he looked at Mum and smiled saying, "Goodnight, and good luck!"

I think Mum was very relieved to get back home safely, but I know she had enjoyed it. She was such a good sport and I was very proud of her.

* * * * * * * * *

The three of us often went out together. Sometimes we

would go, with Grandma, on Sunday afternoon, to Regents Park. We would play ball and I was always surprised to see how well Mum could throw and catch. I think, like me, she would have loved sport if she had had the opportunity.

On other occasions Basil and I would take a boat out on the lake, rowing past Mum and Grandma as they watched from a park bench on the bank. I know that Mum was always happy when she could see that we were enjoying ourselves.

On Bank Holidays, there was always a Fair on Hampstead Heath. I loved it. I never wanted to waste money on sideshows, like the hoop-la or the rifle range. All I wanted was the dangerous exhilarating rides.

"Oh, just one more go, please," I used to beg, and she never said no. I always used to feel a bit guilty about the extra ride, knowing that she could not really afford it, but somehow I think she always expected it.

In the summer, we used to go rambling in the country. There was a weekly item in the Evening Standard newspaper, written by 'Fieldfare', showing a map of the walk, and the total distance, and we used to take a neighbour's dog with us. He lived in Marchmont Street, but he thought he belonged to us and would regularly come to the flat and scratch at the door to be let in.

One of the ten-mile circular walks, called 'Through The Kent Valleys', started in Farnborough, which was one of the villages where Mum had been fostered as a child. We found the house in Station Road and stopped to look at it.

"It hasn't really changed very much in thirty years", she reflected. "It brings it all back to me. I remember how much I hated it."

"Why did you hate it?"

"I don't think she liked me. She was quite cruel, and made me work like a slave. The only thing I had to look forward to was Sunday, when I used to go to Sunday School. And sometimes she even stopped that."

"Why did she stop you going to Sunday School?"

"Because if I stayed at home I could work. I remember one Sunday when I was nearly ready to go, when she said, 'you must clean your shoes before you go', so I went and cleaned them quickly because I didn't want to be late. Then she said, 'You haven't cleaned the backs properly, so you're not going'."

"How old were you when you lived here?" I asked.

"Oh, I can't really remember," said Mum, "about eight or nine, I think."

I couldn't imagine a life in which the highlight of the week was Sunday School, nor that somebody could be so cruel as to ban this simple pleasure.

Illegitimate children were very vulnerable to abuse and exploitation. There was no help or support for unmarried mothers. It was a shameful condition in those days and frequently the mother and her child were ostracised by society. Many babies were abandoned and brought up in orphanages.

Grandma wanted to keep her child but had no home of her own. Her only choice was to place Mum in a foster home and pay for her keep until she was old enough to work with her in service. Many of the women who took in those unwanted children did so only for financial gain and a strong hardworking girl was an asset as she could work in the house and look after other children.

Mum never knew who her father was, nor whether her

brother, Reg, five years younger, had the same father. Grandma never talked about it. He may have been one of the other servants – the gardener or the butler, or a local village boy. Or he may have been the Lord of the Manor (or his son). It was not unknown for men in these privileged positions to expect to have a little fun with a pretty servant girl, without facing up to their responsibilities. We shall never know. All I know is that Grandma was working in a big house in Leicestershire, where they hunted with hounds, and that Grandma kept her job – a reward, perhaps, for being discreet.

Mum's miserable childhood made her determined to love and care for her own children, and to encourage us to follow our education for as long as possible. She wanted a better life for us.

Seeing the house in Farnborough reminded her of the deprivation and misery she had suffered, which was in sharp contrast to the happy family ramble we enjoyed that day 'Through The Kent Valleys'.

GREYHOUND RACING

We didn't go out so often in the winter and there was not much to do at home. You couldn't curl up with a book by the fire because we had no room for an armchair. We could only sit round the table, and the only fire was in the big black kitchen range.

Sometimes in the evening we would play darts or turn the board over and play rings. This meant we had to move the table and chairs over a bit to give us more room. The extra footsteps as we walked backwards and forwards to collect our darts could be heard by Mrs Murphy in the flat below and she would bang on her ceiling with a broomstick. We tried to walk as quietly as possible but when she knocked up for a second time, we knew it was time to stop.

There wasn't much to do, just sitting round the table. Sometimes we played cards. Dad liked to play solo or nap when Uncle Monty came. I was allowed to play only if they needed someone to make up a four. We played for money, but the stakes were low – a halfpenny, penny and twopence. At Christmas we used to play till about five o'clock in the morning, which made me feel very grown-up.

Dad was never a heavy gambler, but he had an account with City Tote, and he used to enjoy an occasional visit to Harringay dog racing. He used to go with his brother Monty and sometimes, I was allowed to go with them.

Uncle Monty used to 'study form' and after writing pages of figures, he was sure he had calculated the winner.

"How much money have you got?" he would ask. "It can't lose. How much have you got?"

"Half-a-crown," I replied, which was my weekly pocket money.

"Give it to me and I'll double it."

It was very tempting. It would be nice to have five shillings.

"It can't lose," he repeated.

I knew that if the dog lost, I would have no pocket money for a week, but he sounded so sure. He was very persistent and I liked the idea of doubling my pocket money. I gave him my half-crown. He put it on 'Mick the Miller' who was running in trap six. The dog paraded past us before the race and my dog looked magnificent in his black and white striped coat. He was strong and muscular and walked with a spring in his step.

It was very exciting and I was optimistic. The dogs were put into their traps, according to the colour of the coat they were wearing, and the electric hare set in motion. The hare went round once on its own, exciting the dogs, and on the next circuit the dogs were released. My heart was thumping and I could understand why so many people came to share this excitement. Mick The Miller was in the lead, and I already had five shillings in my pocket. I jumped up and down, willing him on to stay in front. He was being challenged by the dog in the red coat, from trap one.

"Go on Mick," I shouted as I jumped up and down. He only had to stay in front. He was winning, and I would have five shillings to take home.

The dog in trap one had other ideas, and so did the dogs in traps two and five. They went past him and he came in fourth. It was so disappointing. He had lost and so had I. My week's pocket money had gone. I had learned my lesson. 'A bird in the hand is worth two in the bush'. Don't try to get something for nothing. Don't be greedy. Value what you've got and be satisfied. From that day I have never gambled. I have never been tempted by the promise of a quick profit. I have always been a cautious investor. How different I might have been today if Mick The Miller had won and I had doubled my money, I shall never know. All I know is that in retrospect I am grateful that at Harringay on that Saturday afternoon, I lost.

My interest in dog-racing did not last long. I went a few more times, because it was an opportunity for an outing with my father. I used to watch the dogs being paraded before each race by their kennel-maids, and would try to pick a winner. I would then imagine that I had placed a bet, and kept a mental note of my losses and gains. I soon realised that I was wise to keep my pocket money safe in my pocket. Uncle Monty always said it was 'a mug's game!' but it didn't stop him from gambling. He and Dad were exhilarated when they had backed a winner, and they joined the happy throng of people queuing up to claim their winnings from the bookie. There were, of course, far more people who had lost their stakes, and who were pinning their hopes on the next race.

Backing the winner produced a sense of euphoria and confidence, and the winnings provided the means for a higher stake in the next race. Any gains made had usually disappeared before the end of the meeting. It was definitely 'A Mug's Game!'.

The only other outing I ever had with my father was an occasional trip on a Sunday morning – and it was always the same. We would walk to Holborn Kingsway and catch a number 33 tram. It was quite an exciting ride because it went down the subway with tram-stops underground along the route. I was fascinated by the design of the trams, with a driver's seat at each end. The wooden seats had a heavy hinged back which could be swung across the seat for the return journey, so that you were facing the right way.

The subway passed under Aldwych and Somerset House, and we emerged into daylight by the River Thames. We would take a walk along the embankment before returning home at mid-day. Dad would leave us when we got to the Red Lion in Herbrand Street, and I would go on ahead to find Mum cooking the Sunday dinner. We would eat at two o'clock, when Dad came back from the pub.

These few outings with my father, probably no more than a dozen in all, were almost the only occasions in my childhood when I went out with him. It is true that I accompanied him a few times before the war, when he went to collect his 'dole money' from Pentonville Road, but in general, he took little interest in our activities. I cannot recall any occasion in my life when we went out together as a whole family, nor when my mother and father left the house together.

He was ambitious for us, and was very proud that I was at Grammar School. He believed that education was the key to success and wanted us to do well. There was never any suggestion that any of us should leave school at fourteen, or fifteen, to help the family finances.

My father was very strict, and had no qualms about administering corporal punishment. My mother always tried to protect us, but she too, was frightened to displease him. She accepted his authority over her without question. He had very strong views about how a woman should look and my mother had to wear plain clothes, which were not sexually provocative, and sensible shoes. She was not allowed to have her hair permed, nor to wear lipstick. And he wanted the same rules to apply to me. I had arranged to meet my friend, Donie. We were not going anywhere special, but I just wanted to look 'grown-up'.

"Get that muck off your face before you go out," he shouted, "you look like a prostitute!"

I blotted if off on some soft paper, and removed most of it.

"If you don't get it all off, I'll scrub it off for you."

By the time I had finished washing it off, my mouth and chin looked sore and red.

"You're not going out," he decreed.

"There's no lipstick left," I argued, "It's just red from hard washing."

"You're not going anywhere," he repeated.

"But you said if I took it off …."

"You're not going out, and that's final!"

And once he had issued a veto, ending with 'and that's final', I knew it was no good arguing with him. I didn't want to be on the receiving end of his punishment.

I was not easily deterred and did not give up with my experiments with make-up. I was being influenced by the glamorous film stars of the post-war era – Margaret Lockwood, Patricia Roc, Jean Simmons, and many others, and I wanted to look beautiful. I bought some foundation cream and face powder, and some eye shadow. I did not think Dad could complain if I wore it at home, and I spent many hours sitting at the table with a mirror propped up in front of me, trying to get it right, but without much success.

I was not really a glamorous type – I was much too sporty. I had a stocky build and would always feel much more at home in the gym or on the sports field. It felt quite natural to have a healthy glow, with beads of perspiration and windswept hair, but I did not think that that image would attract a boyfriend. I was very lacking in confidence, which was not helped by Dad's tactless and unkind comments. "A penny for the guy!" he would say with sarcasm if he saw me wearing lipstick, or "what's the matter – have you cut your mouth?" If he saw me putting on a make-up base, he would say, "Don't use it all. You can fill in those cracks in the wall if you've got any left."

Mum could not give me any advice or help in any way as she had never worn make-up, but I so much wanted someone to tell me I looked pretty – or even to say that I looked quite attractive.

The hurtful comments destroyed my self-esteem and took away any confidence I might have had. Perhaps even more important was that it ruined any chance there might have been in having a warm and meaningful relationship with my father.

Six years of separation had taken their toll and in many ways my parents were like strangers. They had not seen me grow up and they didn't really know me. We had lost those years between my childhood and adolescence.

It was to be many years before I felt close to my mother, and the gulf between my father and me was never really bridged.

In spite of this, I had a certain respect for him and was influenced by his opinions. From time to time he would utter words of advice which I accepted without question.

"Keep out of trouble and don't get on the wrong side of the law. Once you've got a police record, you're finished."

On another occasion he advised us to 'get a good job with a pension and stay there, and if you don't agree with the views of the boss, it's best to say nothing'. This explained his attitude of appeasement at the General Election. He would agree with everybody, and wanted everybody to like him.

Another piece of advice was 'Don't have any truck with the Irish. You can never trust them!' He never produced any evidence to support this view, but I believed him because I thought he was always right.

He also seemed to be very knowledgeable about the weather. Before we went out for school in the morning, he would say 'Wrap up well – there's going to be a cold wind,' or 'I think we'll have some rain presently, you'd better take your mac.' It was years before I realised he'd been listening to the weather forecast on the wireless.

Dad also had very strong views on punctuality. He was always up early. He used to go to bed at about eight o'clock in the evening, probably through boredom. There was nothing for him to do in the evening. With no space in the room for an armchair, we just sat around the table. Consequently he was awake hours before the rest of us, and would get up at about five o'clock. When he had finished his breakfast, he would clean all our shoes. Apart from carving the joint of meat for Sunday dinner, which he did regularly, this was the only contribution he ever made in the running of the home.

Then he would sit and read his morning newspaper until it was time to wake the family. While we were busy filling jugs and kettles, and waiting our turn to wash in the kitchen bowl, he would leave for work. "I think I'll be strolling along now," he would say and off he would go. 'Stroll' was a word he often used, and which I always associate with him. I never saw him hurry. He didn't need to. He was always early and he loved to be the first to arrive in his office every morning.

"You'll never get anywhere in life if you can't get there on time," was his advice.

Getting to school on time was not always easy. It was a journey of about six miles and involved going on the underground from Russell Square to Manor House, and then a further two or three miles on a trolley bus to Stamford Hill.

Leaving home at exactly the right time for this long journey was not helped by our very unpredictable kitchen clock. In one sense it was very reliable because we always knew exactly what it was going to do and when it was going to do it. The trouble was that the time it kept was not the same as the rest of the world.

The hands were loose. At about three minutes past the hour, the minute hand would drop forward about seven or eight minutes. So it was always fast on the way down. When it got to the half hour, the minute hand would stay on the six until the mechanism had taken up the slack and then the hand would slowly be dragged to the top again.

Nobody ever tried to tighten the hands, nor suggested that perhaps for a small charge this problem could have been rectified by Joe Proviso, the watch and clock repairer in Marchmont Street. Mr Proviso could always been seen in his window, wearing a magnifying eyeglass as he repaired broken clocks, but ours was not broken and we were used to it. Between us we became quite adept at guessing the time.

"How's the minute hand?" someone would ask, as it pointed to the six and the reply would be either, "Oh, it's only just got there, which meant you had plenty of time, or "It's starting to go up now," which meant you were probably going to be late.

There was always the wireless to listen to and this gave us an accurate time-check on the hour.

The wireless was our major form of entertainment, but that was not without its problems. With no electricity in the flat, we couldn't use mains power. Our wireless was powered by an accumulator. This was a heavy glass jar containing electrodes and filled with acid through which an electric current could be passed to generate electricity. It was rather like a small car battery. Like the flat irons, it was necessary to have two – one in use and one being recharged. This was done at the hardware shop in Marchmont Street and each week we would take one round to the shop, leaving it to be charged, and return with the other.

Sometimes, after excessive use, the accumulator would deteriorate and reception would fade or become distorted in the middle of a programme. Nothing in Peabody Buildings was easy or straightforward.

The strain was intolerable and I wanted to get out.

"Let's go to the Housing Department again," I suggested, "and see if we've moved up on the waiting list. We've been on it for a year. If we remind them, we might get a place quicker."

Again, we were in for a shock and a major disappointment.

"Well, you don't seem to be on our list. What was the name? Matthews?"

"Yes, Matthews."

"I'm sorry, we don't have you on the list yet."

"But we came two years ago and a lady told us to come back in a year to be put on the list. And we came back last year, and a man took all our details and said he was going to put us on the list. We thought that we would have moved up by now."

The lady took our details all over again but she was not very encouraging.

"There are so many people who have priority and they must be housed first."

"Are we priority?" I asked, "I'm nearly fifteen and I have to share a room with my two brothers – one is ten and the other is already eighteen."

"Well, I know it must be difficult for you, and I've put you on the list, but you don't qualify as 'Priority'."

"How long to you think it will be?" I asked despondently.

"I can't really say. It could be two or three years – or even longer – I really don't know. So much of London has got to be re-built, and that's going to take a long time. We are having to put a lot of people in temporary accommodation while they wait for a proper house."

Prefabricated houses – 'prefabs', and Nissen huts were being erected all over the city. They were constructed in the factories and delivered to the site on a lorry to be assembled very quickly.

They didn't look very attractive, particularly from the outside, but they could be made to feel very homely. Billie's sister Dorothy lived in one and it was very comfortable. The plasterboard walls could be papered or painted and if you hung a few pictures and arranged some ornaments, you felt you were in a proper house. And of course, they had all the necessary supplies of water and electricity, and sanitation. I would have loved to have moved to a prefab, but not being considered priority, we didn't qualify for one. There was nothing to do but wait.

THE LONG TERM EFFECTS

The years were passing and there was still no hope of being re-housed. Our visits to the Town Hall were never encouraging. It hardly seemed worth asking. We went there from time to time, hoping that by reminding them of our plight, our housing application would be considered favourably. It was unbearable, sharing a bedroom with the boys, and the living area seemed to shrink as we were growing.

The lack of toilet facilities was a great embarrassment and I was back with a po under the bed. I felt ashamed of living in Peabody Buildings. This was aggravated at the time by a very popular radio show starring Jimmy Edwards, called 'Take It

From Here', in which he coined a 'catch phrase' …… 'Back to the Buildings'. There were, of course, other blocks of flats which were 'Buildings', but the term 'The Buildings' was synonymous with Peabody. Jimmy's catch phrase was regularly included in the script, and everyone was familiar with it. If you were required to give your address, and I said 'Peabody Buildings', some joker would laugh and say 'Back to the Buildings'. The name plaque on the wall was 'Herbrand Street Estate' to distinguish it from the many Peabody blocks all over London, easily recognised by their identical architecture. I decided to give my address as 8A Herbrand Street Estate, but I don't suppose that many people were fooled.

My one consolation was that there were no Peabody Estates near my school. They could be seen in Hammersmith, Holborn, Elephant & Castle, and alongside the railway tracks as you left the main line stations of King's Cross, Paddington and Victoria. There were none, as far as I knew, near my school in Stamford Hill, nor in the immediate area. When I was at school, I could forget Peabody and regain a little of my self-respect and confidence. I thought I was probably worrying unnecessarily about this, as those friends who knew where I lived were not much better off than I was, and would not think less of me for living there.

I was doing well at school, particularly in the field of sport. I was often games captain of my class, and played regularly in all the school teams – netball, hockey, tennis and rounders, and was an accomplished gymnast. These achievements commanded respect and I was happy at school. My commitment to games was always one hundred per cent, regardless of whether it was in a school match, a championship or just a class games lesson.

Tuesday June 3rd, 1947 was a very hot day and our afternoon lesson was games. The winter sports of netball and hockey had given way to tennis and rounders, and with no sports field attached to the school we had to walk to a small field in Egerton Road, about half a mile away.

I was the bowler in my rounders team and Betty Law was playing backstop (which is like wicket-keeper). The game is similar to cricket in that the batsman can be caught out by the fielding team.

One of the balls which I bowled clipped the edge of Barbara Walker's rounders stick and went straight up in the air. Betty and I both ran forward looking up to catch the ball and collided face to face. She was an inch or two shorter than I was and I think I hit my nose on her forehead. The bang on my nose made my eyes run, but I was not crying. Betty was!

We stopped the game and I was taken over to the edge of the field to sit on the bank in the shade. I wanted to carry on playing.

"Barbara's out!" I claimed, "I caught her out, I've still got the ball in my hand!"

Nobody took any notice of what I was saying. Miss Rapp looked at me and said, "I think you'd better go to hospital." My eyes were still watering and Miss Rapp must have thought I was crying, and as I was not the sort of person who would cry, she may have thought I had a bad headache and needed medical attention.

"I'm all right," I insisted, "It's just that my eyes keep watering. And if we carry on playing, Barbara's out."

"Just sit there quietly in the shade," she said, "Miss Defty has gone to call an ambulance."

It seemed a lot of unnecessary fuss but I had no choice. I let go of the ball and watched it roll down the bank.

"Well, she's out anyway," I repeated, still hoping that our team would win.

The ambulance arrived and Miss Defty accompanied me to the Prince of Wales Hospital in Tottenham. I could not understand why Betty wasn't here as well because she was definitely crying. I was taken to the waiting room in 'Accident and Emergency' where it was very, very hot.

A nurse came over to where we were sitting and Miss Defty explained that I had had a collision whilst playing rounders. The nurse looked at me and asked "Is that a result of the accident or has it always been like that?"

Like what?" I asked.

"No," said Miss Defty, "that is a result of the accident."

"What is?" I asked in panic, "What's wrong? I want a mirror! Have you got a mirror, please?"

"I'll see if I can find one," said the nurse, and she went and fetched one. I looked in the mirror and was horrified with what I saw. My nose looked as if was flat on the side of my face. I could see that it was broken and I looked ugly. "Will it go back?" I asked in alarm, "Or will I always look like this?" Now I really did want to cry. I couldn't face life with a face like this. I looked stupid with a flattened nose.

"You'll be all right," said the nurse, "the Doctor will see you very quickly and they'll have it back in no time. They'll give you a general anaesthetic so you won't feel a thing."

The doctor confirmed that a small operation would put things right, but that they could not give a general anaesthetic without parental consent. We had no telephone and Mum was six miles away. Someone would have to go and tell her. Someone was going to have to go to Peabody Buildings and see where I lived.

"Can't I sign it myself?" I pleaded, "It will take Mum hours to get here. I live near Russell Square. Mum wouldn't mind if I signed it. I'm fifteen now. I had my birthday last week. I don't want to wait two or three hours and Mum might not be in anyway. She has to go to work." What I really meant was 'I don't want anyone to see where I live. I don't want them to know that we live in the slums.' I was deeply ashamed of living in Peabody Buildings and did not want anyone to go there. School and home were two separate places and I wanted to keep them apart. I was happy when I was at school. I could forget my poor home and I felt on equal terms with my friends, many of whom lived in beautiful houses, and I didn't want anyone to see mine.

"I'm sorry," they said, "you're not old enough to sign. You'll have to wait for your mother."

"I expect they'll ask Miss Cunningham to go," said Miss Defty, "She goes your way, doesn't she, so it won't be out of her way." Miss Cunningham lived near Earls Court, and she was the only teacher I ever saw on the train in the morning. She was young and very attractive, and she taught mathematics which was my favourite subject. Sometimes I would sit with her on the train and she was always very friendly. She would not be able to call on Mother until the end of afternoon school It was going to be a long wait.

The waiting room was unbearably hot. Another patient came and sat opposite me with the early evening newspaper. The headlines were:

263

'93° IN THE SHADE'

It was the hottest day for many years. I sat there still wearing my games kit, waiting for Mum to arrive.

I could imagine Miss Cunningham getting off the train at Russell Square and looking for Herbrand Street – and then she would see The Buildings. She would have to walk up the two flights of stone stairs in 'A' Block to number 8 and knock on the door. I didn't think she would have to go in - at least I hoped not. When people came to the door we never asked them to come in, we would talk to them at the door. But even if Miss Cunningham stayed on the landing, she would be able to see the public sink and the lavatory, so she would know we hadn't got one inside.

I had always believed that I lived far enough away from school to be able to conceal my shame and now Miss Cunningham was going to knock on my door. I felt ashamed and humiliated. I thought she would think less of me and look down on me. She knew I was good at Maths and was always near the top of the class in the exams. I found the subject easy and did not have to work very hard to understand it. Now that she has seen where I lived, I thought she would have a different view of me..

I wondered if she would say anything to the other teachers. Well – I wouldn't know and I couldn't do anything about it anyway, but I would not be able to sit with her on the train. I wouldn't know what to say. I could get in the last compartment to avoid her. At least I knew she would not say anything about me to the pupils – to my friends. That would be unbearable.

Billie knew of course. She lived in Cookham Buildings in the East End and they were nearly as bad. They had a kitchen sink with running water and they had their own indoor toilet, but there were eight of them in three bedrooms and I knew she wouldn't say anything about my home.

I sat in the sweltering heat for nearly three hours turning all this over in my mind and worrying about my face.

Finally, Mum arrived hot and worried, and signed the consent form for my operation. It was all over very quickly and was quite painless and I was able to go home. I stayed away from school for the rest of the week and after a few days of severe bruising my face returned to normal.

The doctor had made a wonderful job of repairing the damage to my face but it was to be many years before I recovered from the pain and humiliation caused by our appalling living conditions.

Sadly the reputation of Peabody was widely known. Mavis took me aside one day and said, "Some of the girls were talking about you today, behind your back, and criticising you for living in Peabody Buildings. I was appalled," she said, "and I stuck up for you. I told them 'You mustn't judge a person by where they live, you must judge them by their personal qualities – and June's as good as any of us'."

Mavis was a very honest person, and very fair. I was grateful to her for defending me, and for reprimanding those who had been criticising me. But my shame and humiliation was known at school, and it confirmed my worst fear – that people do actually think less of you, if you live in a slum.

Her words stayed with me, and I went over them again and again in my mind. Who, I wondered, had started the conversation? I knew Mavis would not tell me. Who was it that was looking down on me? And the others, who had been listening, did they agree with Mavis, or did they, too, now look down on me and despise me? I tried to guess who the girls were, and whenever I spoke to someone I thought, 'was it you?'. Someone thought I was low, and now I was beginning to feel very low. Mavis was right to defend me, but I so wished that she hadn't told me.

Sometime after this I sprained my ankle playing netball, and I had to go to hospital to have it X-rayed. I sat in the crowded waiting room at Charing Cross Hospital, until it was my turn. "Next please," they called, and I limped over to the desk.

"Name?" she asked.

"June Matthews, spelt with two T's," I replied clearly. People often spelt our surname incorrectly.

"Date of birth?"

"Twenty eighth of May, 1932," I replied as she filled in the form.

"Address?" I could feel myself beginning to blush. I leaned forward over the counter and spoke quietly so that the people in the waiting room would not hear.

"8A Herbrand Street Estate."

"Pardon?" she said. I repeated it. "Is that Peabody Buildings?" she enquired.

"Yes," I admitted. I could never escape the shame and humiliation of my background. People always wanted to know your address, and as soon as they knew it, they looked down on you. What I did not know at the time – and it was better not to know – was that we would not be re-housed until 1952, when I was twenty. We had to wait seven years and even then we escaped only on my father's health grounds. He had suffered a number of heart attacks and a doctor's certificate advised that he should not climb stairs. His medical condition transferred our housing application to the 'Priority List'.

My teenage years had been ruined. I would not take a boyfriend home, I was too ashamed. It was easier to end a relationship.(Sorry Len!).

There were happy times, of course, and successes – the greatest was in being selected to play netball for Middlesex County and the England Team in its first post-war season.

These achievements helped to see me through those dark years. I had expected so much. For six long years during the war, I had waited to go home. I had waited for the Bluebirds with the promise of 'love and laughter, and peace ever after'.

Well, we had peace, and my mother's love sustained us throughout the misery, but there wasn't much laughter. I had survived more or less unscathed from a six-year war. Or had I? I have one small scar as evidence of physical damage. This was the result of a piece of glass about the size of a sultana being hidden in a new coir mat which had been ordered by the school for the P.E.department. When landing awkwardly in the gym after vaulting over the horse, I ended up on my knees with the glass embedded in my shin. Apparently the mat had been stored in a warehouse which had been bombed shattering all the windows. The splinter of glass was eventually removed at Great Ormond Street Hospital where I suffered the indignity of having an anti-tetanus injection in my buttocks.

I was lucky in that none of my immediate family was lost or injured although my future father-in-law lost an arm when his home was bombed and I was never to meet my youngest brother-in-law who was killed on active service in the battlefields in

Normandy. My son Alan researched the postings of his uncle's regiment through the Commonwealth War Graves Commission and then took us to see the grave. He is buried in a beautifully kept cemetery in Hottot – Les – Bagues near Bayeux. I was very moved to see the white headstone engraved 'STANLEY GEORGE PARKINS, AGED 19', and as I stood so close to a family member I reflected on the futility of war. I thought of Rupert Brookes poem 'The Soldier',

> *"If I should die, think only this of me:*
> *That there's some corner of a foreign field*
> *That is for ever England."*

Stanley was one of many boys in that cemetery and there are numerous cemeteries – so many wasted lives. I know this had a profound effect on my husband.

And what about me? I was happy in Radwell but I lost six years with my family which could never be replaced. My parents – and my brothers – did not see me grow up. And when we were eventually reunited our attempts to re-establish family bonds were thwarted by our appalling living conditions. We would no doubt have been re-housed much sooner if there had not been such a severe housing shortage after the bombing.

My teenage years were without question the unhappiest days of my life – the only unhappy ones, - and I still look back on them with sadness and anger, and with much resentment. We lived in squalor and I felt contaminated. In recent years the flats have been modernised and are desirable places in which to live. The estates in central London are well situated, close to theatres and museums and are convenient for West End shopping. Some of the apartments are now privately owned and there is no longer a stigma attached to living there. But for me, living there was a painful experience and it left its scars. It was years before I could openly admit to having lived in Peabody Buildings. Now after nearly sixty years, when my behaviour is less than perfect, I can enjoy a joke with my children and we say "You can take the girl out of Peabody but you can't take Peabody out of the girl!" Or they might whisper to me "Mum, don't let them guess that you came from Peabody!". I have come a long way but I can't claim that I survived the war unscathed.

I had waited for my Bluebird, but when my bird came, it was an albatross. I felt cheated and disillusioned, and I looked back to my carefree days in Radwell with longing and nostalgia. In spite of the war I had been happy there. I wanted to go back, where I would be able to see the sky and hear the birds singing. I wanted to go back to the green fields and open spaces, and I know that one day I will return.

EPILOGUE

'The Homecoming'

'Dig the grave and let me lie.'

R L Stevenson   Requiem

It is now seventy years since I first saw Radwell and it has changed remarkably little during that time. The Village Hall still stands opposite Rose Cottages (now with a telephone box outside it) and the Council Cottages - now called Radwell Cottages - look exactly the same. Pebble Cottages have retained their picturesque appearance and the pretty lane winds its way down the hill past Radwell Farm and the church to the lake, with the magnificent view of the old Mill House on the far side. One or two new houses have appeared but there have been no major building developments in the village.

Mains water and drainage were connected after the war and the well and pump remain only as reminders of a bygone age. The yew trees which flank the path to All Saints Church are noticeably much bigger. During the last sixty years I have made many visits to Radwell. I am drawn there like a homing pigeon. I have keys to the Village Hall so I can make myself a cup of tea, and also to the church. It was locked for a short while after a burglary but is now usually open.

In the little churchyard I found the grave of Auntie Edie and Uncle 'erbert. I was shocked to discover that Auntie had died aged 64 only 6 months after I left Radwell – she was 60 at the outbreak of war when she opened her home to John and me. After her death, Uncle 'erbert lived with his son for eighteen years and was then brought back to be reunited with his wife in the corner of the churchyard.

In 1995 I applied successfully to the Diocese of St Albans to reserve a gravespace for myself. I met The Rev. Stephen Pugh, the priest in charge, to identify the plot. He told me to choose where I would like to go. I wandered around looking at the grassy areas like someone looking for the greenest, most weed-free spot to have a picnic, or to pitch a tent for the night. This was going to be a very long night so I wanted it to be right.

We eventually agreed on a plot 'South of Mrs Jarosz and east of John Smith'. I was overwhelmed by the significance of this apparently simple decision. Would I really be lowered into the ground at this spot some time in he future? How many years from now? Would my grandchildren be grown up?

Three weeks later I received a 'Faculty for Gravespace Reservation' in my name bearing the seal of the Diocese of St Albans. It was tied with green ribbon and included a plan of Radwell Churchyard showing a rectangle outlined in red bearing the words 'Reserved for JUNE PARKINS'.

In my final letter of thanks to the Diocese I concluded 'I am finding the idea of being buried at Radwell quite exciting and very comforting, although I am in no great hurry to take up residence'.

Well, one day I will be taking up residence and they will be waiting for me again in the village hall. This time I will not be arriving in a coach with a label round my neck as I had in 1939, but in ceremonious style in a hearse. This time it will not be the ladies of the village who will be waiting for me offering me sanctuary for the duration of the war, it will be my family and friends who have come to say goodbye as I make my final journey home to rest permanently in peace.

There will be tea and biscuits for everyone in the village hall followed by a short and, I hope, not too gloomy service in the beautiful little village church All Saints. And after I have been lowered into my final resting place, only a few yards away from Uncle 'erbert and Auntie Edie, my friends and family will be able to go on their way cheerfully, knowing that the evacuee has returned happily to her spiritual home.

Under the wide and starry sky
Dig the grave and let me lie
Glad did I live and gladly die
And I laid me down with a will
This be the verse you grave for me
Here he lies where he longed to be
Home is the sailor, home from the sea
And the hunter home from the hill.

R L Stevenson

* * * * * * * * *